NEGROPHOBIA

ARE YOU NEGROPHOBIC?
Study the Picture Below

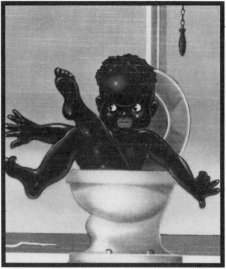

A) Do you blush with embarrassment and *snigger* behind splayed fingers?

B) Does your mouth water for a handful of those chocolate figurines you ate as a child?

C) Do you feel as if the lives lost in the four-hundred-year struggle against racist oppression and the hours spent raising the community's consciousness of its revolutionary potential was a complete waste of time?

D) Do you see through its transparently suggestive subliminal mechanism (devil's food darkness *rimmed* by porcelain white), convinced it's a racially subversive trick to lure young, supple-bodied white women into bed with nickel-eyed negroes?

E) Are you overcome with a cold, sweating, and unrelenting fear that a band of African pygmies is going to creep in through your bedroom window tonight and attack you with poisoned darts?

If you answered Yes to any of the above questions, you are one of the many unfortunate and chronic sufferers of negrophobia (ne'-gre-fo'-bea) n. 1) A strong aversion to the presence of negroes. 2) A persistent, exaggerated, and wholly irrational fear or dread of negroes. 3) The story of Bubbles Brazil, a girl trapped in a world without white folks.

NEGROPHOBIA

An Urban Parable

A Novel

Darius James

St. Martin's Press
New York

NEGROPHOBIA. Copyright © 1992 by Darius James. All rights reserved.
Printed in the United States of America. No part of this book may be
used or reproduced in any manner whatsoever without written permission
except in the case of brief quotations embodied in critical articles or reviews.
For information, address St. Martin's Press, 175 Fifth Avenue, New York,
N.Y. 10010.

Photo page 1 courtesy Doris Kloster.
Insert illustrations 1 and 2 courtesy Joy Glidden; photo 3 courtesy Doris Kloster.

Originally published by Citadel Press, 1992
Portions of *Negrophobia* have previously appeared in *Between C & D: Lower
Eastside Fiction, Peau Sensible, Tribes,* and *The Bahlasti Papers.*

Library of Congress Cataloging-in-Publication Data

James, Darius.
    Negrophobia / Darius James.
        p.   cm.
    ISBN 0-312-09350-0
    1. Racism—United States—Fiction.   2. Afro-Americans—Fiction.
I. Title.
PS3560.A37887N4   1993
813'.54—dc20   93-17422
                                                                              CIP

First Paperback Edition: August 1993

10 9 8 7 6 5 4 3 2 1

To Joy Glidden,
who more than my loas made the completion
of this book possible;
to my father,
Walter Edward James,
who made me possible;
and to my sister,
Jeri Collette James,
who laughs at all my jokes

"Jim, the whole history of this republic is the rape of a white woman and the lynching of a nigger. Those two images."

"You're speaking of images."

"Images my ass. I'm speaking on reality. That's what makes this swirl go around. The lynching of niggers and the raping of women."

Steve Cannon
"Looney Tunes Under a
Deep Blue Moon"

Minister Louis Farrakhan: The young lady said she's afraid of violence. And isn't sad that we, who have been the victims of so much violence—now, whites fear violence from us. We do not have a history of killing white people. White people have a history of killing us.

And what you fear—may I say this, sir? What you fear—and it's a deep guilt thing that white folks suffer—you are afraid that if we ever come to power, we will do to you and your fathers what you and your people have done to us. And I think you are *judging us by the state of your own mind,* and that is not necessarily the mind of black people.

Donahue: And we'll be back in just a moment.

"Donahue,"
March 14, 1990
Show #0314–90

...sooner or later being less human leads the oppressed to struggle against those who made them so. In order for this struggle to have meaning, the oppressed must not, in seeking to regain their humanity (which is a way to create it), become in turn oppressors of the oppressors, but rather restorers of the humanity of both.

This, then, is the great humanistic and historical task of the oppressed: to liberate themselves and their oppressors as well.

—Paulo Freire, "Pedagogy of the Oppressed"

Sometimes I think this whole world is a big sharecropper's shack. Some of us are niggers. And the rest of us are black.

—Michael O'Donoghue

Voodoo is magick's African face in the West. Radical, transformative, and visionary, voodoo is a unique weapon of the imagination. Its rites, rituals, and spellcastings are techniques designed to stimulate the right-lobe functions of the brain—the center of dreams, poetry, spirit, intuition, and sexuality—and so provide its devotees with a powerful creative vehicle for pushing beyond conventional modes of being into the self's dangerous terrain.

What occurs on the magickal level of voodoo is subliminal. It begins below the threshold of consciousness, in the subconscious, the seat of archetypes and emotions, our primal past.

Imagine the difference between conscious and subconscious as the difference between foreground and background. The foreground is detail. The background is pattern. Consciousness sees the tree. The subconscious sees the forest.

By manipulating magickal archetypes and symbols, a stereoscopic effect is created from the conscious and subconscious, manifesting a supraconscious.

Voodoo is a religion, but not a centralized one. Its acts are personalized—mutating, changing shape, adapting to their particular time and locale.

As a result, present-day urban America has spawned a new generation of loa out of concrete and steel, out of radio and TV, out of comics and film. The new loa are invoked by beat-box rhythm, Burroughsian cutup, industrial music, and the extreme edges of performance art.

Malcolm X is celebrated as a new loa in the Petro pantheon.

In the Western mind, rooted as it is in rationalism and Christian dogma, a dichotomy exists between Europe and Africa. Europe represents the foreground of the conscious. Africa is the repository of all that is vile, unspeakable, and taboo in the dark subconscious.

When the "detail" of the European conscious is reconciled with the "patterns" of the African subconscious, the cultural consequences for the Western mind will be devastating....

—Doctor Snakeskin
The Blackman's Guide to Seducing White Women With the Amazing Power of Voodoo

OPEN ON:

INT. Brownstone in Manhattan's Upper West Side—Bedroom—Dawn.

EXTREME CLOSE-UP OF A JOINT balanced on the rim of a silver ashtray. With cigarette paper the color of beach-bleached bone, twisted rather than rolled, and winding with arteries of thin black wrinkles emphasized in shadow, the joint looks like a shriveled, mummified cock stained by a ring of red lipstick. The camera pans along its length with lingering affection.

SFX: The joint's sizzle is amplified, punctuated by the sound of pot seeds popping.

The ashtray rests on a mahogany nightstand with amorphous blots of light shivering across its surface. Set beside the ashtray is an open crescent-shaped box, all lace frills and gilded paper. Its star-stamped lid is embossed with the words:

Min. Louis Farrakhan's "Ambrosia of Islam"
Do-for-Self Designer Chocolates
"Allah eats 'em! And you will too!"

In a profusion of fluted-paper-coffins, spilling over the sides of the box, and lying scattered across the tabletop, are several fez-capped, frog-faced fudge figurines. Each leering figurine bears the likeness of the Honorable Elijah Muhammad. He clutches candy genitalia in tiny fudge fists. Spurts of white chocolate fleck his thighs.

The twisted paper's luminous white, the ashtray's silver glint, and the gilded foil of the candy box are in sharp contrast to the bedroom's enveloping darkness.

3

The camera follows the joint's curling, serpentine ribbons of smoke in a slow, upward tilt. The shot is held in midair as the gathering curls of smoke form the title in exotic lettering:

NEGROPHOBIA

The title dissipates in the darkness. Dolly through smoke and gloam. Stop on a pair of charred, sequined Come-Fuck-Me Shoes hanging at the end of a ribbon draped over a nail. A dried long-stemmed rose is hooked on the head of the nail, its petals splayed like an open vulva.

The cloud of reefer smoke thins to a gray haze, and the disembodied voice of a TEENAGE GIRL is heard, modulated in tones from pot lethargic to speed-freak frantic:

DRUG-ADDLED TEENAGE GIRL
(v.o.)

On my thirteenth birthday, after recovering from the awful discovery that Transvestite Rock was not the hottest happening in puberty since wet dreams...

Come-Fuck-Me's dissolve in the gloam.

The camera pans across a pair of large lips air-brushed on the wall. The lips are pouty and negroid with a touch of tongue, tooth, and saliva.

As the pan draws to a close, the camera betrays a pair of slender vampire canines protruding from the painted mouth.

Dissolve to smoke and gloam. The smoke churns with tumultuous effect. A mob of unruly *Rocky-Horror* cultists appear in a Montage of Polaroid prints, turning in slow

4

pixilated stages from murky gray smudge to a clear color image: pudding-soft PUBESCENTS in glittering Come-Fuck-Me Shoes wearing tight denim cutoffs, slit along the seams, revealing inverted V's of pale thigh. With bosoms bobbing under swastika-emblazoned valentine T's, the PUBESCENTS tease beneath the marquee of New York City's 8th Street Playhouse

Young wet mouths fall on pedestrian necks. Fangs flash. Flesh rips. Crimson rivulets spill from the corners of the girls' mouth in sparkling tear-shaped droplets.

DRUG-ADDLED TEENAGE GIRL
(v.o.)

I burned my Rocky-Horror Picture Show
paraphernalia, sequined Come-Fuck-Me Shoes
and all....

Dissolve to smoke and gloam. Tilt down the surface of a mirror. The oval mirror is set in an ornate bronze frame adorned with raised images of pagan bacchanalia. A candle flame's reflection flickers in the mirror's left-hand corner.

Over-the-shoulder shot of TEEN SEX-BOMB BLONDE. The BLONDE draws a figure eight on her face with a stick of silver greasepaint.

The face in the glass is an uncommon one in the world of the wakeful. It's a face seen in the soup of sleep. A face that surfaces in a stew of haunted imagery. A face of fevered dreams.

The face suggests a breed of cat deified in the temples of ancient Egypt. And if the doctrines of karma and reincarnation were true, they would account for the look of haughtiness about the bow-shaped mouth. The hair is an abundance of lemon-cream curls, with the tip of each tinted a cotton-candy pink. Two braids entwined with strips of leather sprout from each side of the forehead. The almond eyes are large and lynxlike, refracting light in colors from pale green to ice silver. The nose curves to a soft, elfin point, its right nostril pierced with a slender gold ring.

Softness swells the heart. Blood bloats the groin.

DRUG-ADDLED TEENAGE GIRL
(v.o.)

> ...and became a real sixties-era, alienated-from-pig-values, tuned-into-K–OZMIK FM-radio freek. I was no phony weekend hippie. I was bona fide. I sucked off Jerry Garcia.

The BLOND BOMB paints in the figure eight until the ovals on her face are two solid disks. She stands and puts on a pair of black Wayfarer shades, posing before the mirror.

The camera tilts up the reflection in the glass. The BLOND BOMB wears cleated Dr. Martens marked with anarchosatanic symbols in metallic paintpen. Adhesive black Spandex clings to her sturdy athletic legs and outlines her protuberant pudendum. Her graffiti-scratched black leather jacket is ornamented with chrome studs, razor blades, and used syringes. Her puffy pink areolas peek through the shredded curtain of her black T held together by a confusion of safety pins.

DRUG-ADDLED TEENAGE GIRL
(v.o.)

> Then I improved m'moves, switched m'grooves, an' sleazed into a pair of snakeskinned voodoo hooves. I got th'drop on bop. I let m'fingas pop. I became th'girl th'worl' couldn't stop. I was the baby blon' th'boys couldn't con. I was th'one everybody tried to hit on.

> I was wicked white heat from cheek to feet. I'd throw you in a state of agitated doggie heat. I'd make you dream 'n' steam then cream 'n' y'jeans

6

'cause I was the reigning queen supreme of the
cover-girl wet dream.

Stop tilt on face for head shot. The girl in the glass smiles at
her reflection, stroking her cheek with the blunt edge of an
open pearl-handled straight razor.

DRUG-ADDLED TEENAGE GIRL
(v.o.)

My name is Bubbles. Bubbles Brazil. I have a
heart of gold. My blond mons of venus is clipped
and shaped like a golden valentine.

Lick it lovingly...

Bubbles folds the straight razor and drops it into her jacket's
inside pocket. Dolly in for close shot of Bubbles' face.

On the final two syllables of the last line, Bubbles voice dips
on the first syllable and rises on the second.

BUBBLES

You can never be *too cool!*

FADE

INT. Brownstone—Kitchen—Morning.

Close-up on a chunky, brown-faced, kerchief-headed woman grinning from a cylindrical box of Savanna Sal's Hominy Grits.

Pull back and reveal a hefty black arm, with sagging, hamhock-shaped biceps, stirring a thick white brew in a black cast-iron pot.

SFX: A series of short, farting bursts as grits boil and bubble.

As the ladle is lifted from the pot, two pudgy fingers pinch a live white mouse by the tip of its tail, dangling it over the rising wisps of steam. The mouse is casually dropped into the pot of bubbling grits.

With its tiny pink feet paddling frantically, the agonized mouse squeals, vomits blood, and dies. The ladle is placed back into the pot and stirring resumes. The dead mouse sinks beneath the surface of the grits.

Black woman's mouth into view. Her gums are dark chocolate. Her teeth are canary yellow.

BLACK MOUTH

> When 'at boy gwine learn his sef some sense? Ah
> done tol' 'at boy messin' wif dem whyte gals gwine
> a git 'im kil.

Camera pulls back and reveals a monstrous, mammy-sized cookie jar of a woman with doughy animal features and crazed incandescent eyes. Her nappy bleached-blond Afro is a crown of spiky thorns matted with sweat and splashed with splots of Day-Glo colors. Her face and arms are splotched

8

with leaflike patches of missing melanin. The twirl of brown and pink stripes on her left arm resembles the markings of a tiger's coat. A pair of mascara lobster claws wing her eyes.

As the MAID talks on the telephone, she stirs the brew of grits, cradling the telephone's mouthpiece between the underside of her chin and the cleft of her shoulder. An open pancake box, a batter-spattered mixing bowl, and fish entrails are seen on the nearby counter.

MAID
(talking into telephone)

Jus' don' listen. Head hard as a rock. He knowed wha' happen' t'his Unca Lemmie down in Georgia wif dat young whyte gal.

Yas, chile. Dem fool crackas strung 'im up, gutted 'im lak a pig, 'n' bar-be-cued his black b'hine. Dey stood 'round smackin' dey lips, talkin' 'bout *"Gimme 'notha dem greasy nigga ribs!"*

Ah don' know! You tell me what dat ol' snagga-mouf, buck-eye coon want wif a young one? Broke-dick nigga couldn't get his dick hard *since 1926!*

Saw dat young whyte gal's pussy—*Hard dick f'daze!*

Ol' wrinkle-ass *huffin' 'n' hunchin' nigga* what said he only meant to rub it f'luck 'cause dat young whyte gal's pussy look jus' like d'top of a nigga's *haid!*

Chicken-rustlin' rascal.

Nah, dat Weefee ridin' 'round wif dat car load o' whyte gals, can't tell dat nigga nuffin'. He be talkin' 'bout slick skull game, how he be hard on his ho's, keep a big roll in his pocket, 'n' d'res' ob dat ol' okeydoke!

9

Ah oughts t'go out dere mysefs 'n' take a switch to dat citified country nigga's—*great gugga-mugga!*

The Maid's eyes are disks of suprise. Her mouth is an O of wonder.

Bubbles enters the kitchen, sits at the table, and stares at the pancakes piled on the plate in front of her. Hundreds of fish eyes fried inside stare back.

The Maid glares at the ovals on Bubbles's face.

Smiling in mock innocence, Bubbles reaches into her jacket's side pocket, and eats, one by one, a handful of the human-shaped chocolate figurines. Webs of masticated chocolate pop in her mouth.

MAID
(talking into telephone)
Lucille, I'm'a hasta call y'back later.

The Maid hangs the telephone on the wall.

MAID
Miss Bubbas Brasil! What is dat devilish mess caked on yo' face?!

BUBBLES
Magically converging uteri to equalize the balance of my aura's negative and positive energies.

MAID
Mah'uta—*wha'?*

BUBBLES
War paint.

10

MAID

Why can't you dream up sum'in practica'—*like
how ah kin hit d'numba!*

BUBBLES

What's a white girl to do in a school full of
jigaboos?

MAID

Mind her business. Yo' parents spent all dat
money sendin' yo butt off to fancy private schools.
'N' whatchoo do? *Getcha hot little boll-daga ass
throwed out!!* 'N' den you end up in a crazy house
fo' rich dope fiends! Face it, you is jus' gon' hafta
put up wid dem niggas.

Bubbles wrinkles her nose.

BUBBLES

But they're gross and they spit!

A half-eaten nigger baby spits from her mouth.

MAID

Spit back at 'em.

BUBBLES

But you don't know what it's like! Girls yank my
hair and guys yank my tits! That place is a
fucking Monkey House!

She eats another nigger baby.

11

Jigaboos!

Bubbles folds her arms across her breasts and pouts.

MAID

Lookie here, *Miss Whyte 'n' Mighty!!* In dis kitchen, whyte is right if it kin kick *three hundred 'n' sixty pounds of sweatin' black ass!*

Ah don' takes kindly t'you 'ferrin' t'my peepus as jigaboos! You makes us out t'sound like we be hidin' in d'bushes affa dark wif our teef shinin' 'n' shit.

BUBBLES

Coons hide in the bushes after dark with their teeth shining. Jigaboos *steal chickens!*

The Maid lifts the ladle from the pot of sputtering grits. And swings. Bubbles ducks. The Maid misses. The grits slap against the wall, and begin to congeal into frightening glacial forms.

MAID

Don't sass-mouf me!

BUBBLES
(pouting)

Well, it's true…

MAID

Lookie here. Nah dat we is no longa cullid, we is whatchoo calls Neo-African Americans—*hostages* misplaced in time, captives of a racist hist'ry 'n' a oppressed peepus dissolvin' in d'stomach acids of whyte amerika—*d'cause o' so much bad breffs!*

12

BUBBLES

Monkey chatter! I'm oppressed! But you wouldn't know anything about that. You were never *white and pretty!*

MAID

'N' you was never black 'n' broke!

BUBBLES

Thank God! I don't know what I would do without my mane of golden fairy-tale curls!!

MAID

'N' ah bets you be wonnerin' why dem niggas be bustin' you' b'hine all d'time!

BUBBLES

I don't wonder. *I know.*

MAID

If'n you knows so much, what put d'idea in yo' head t'put dat mess on yo' face in d'first place?

BUBBLES

One of your books.

The Maid's eyes ignite into twin lights of paranoia.

MAID

Which books?

BUBBLES

The creepy ones.

The Maid's voice is taut with anger.

MAID

Which "creepy ones"?

BUBBLES

The ones you buy from the Puerto Ricans. *How to
Cause Constipation, Protection From the Evil Eye,
Black Herman's Book of Shrunken Talking Heads...*

The Maid's temper blows with the blistering heat of steam
spouting from a teakettle.

MAID

You been messin' in my mojos! Ah tol' you 'bout bein'
in my books! Dems my sacred books 'n' not fo'
d'eyes o' whyte folks! Ah'ma whips d'hoodoos on
you fo' sho'!

The Maid springs for Bubbles' throat, her fingers curled and
clutching. As her mandarin-curled fingernails near Bubbles'
throbbing jugular, she freezes. She stands eerily immobile.

The Maid's eyes spin around their rims in dizzying circles,
turning up in their sockets until only the whites are visible.
Her tongue flops out of her mouth, contorting one way and
then the other. Beads of sweat pop out on her forehead. Her
head snaps back and forth. Her shoulders hunch and jerk.

MAID

Ah'ma hang d'gris-gris 'bove yo' do'! Snakes
gwine crawl 'cross yo' flo'! D'rats gwine howl 'n'
blood gwine run down yo' jo'! Yo' body gwine
bust out in nasty so's! Yo' ass gwine shrivel up 'n'
you ain't gwine shit no mo'!

Bubbles' eyes widen in awe. She has never seen such a looned
coon.

The Maid slithers into a convulsive snake dance, foams at the mouth, and tears off her clothes. Sweat clings to the hairs of her armpits. Fish-eyed pancakes are slung Frisbee-style across the kitchen. Bruce Lee's kung fu cat cries mingle with James Brown's R&B funk shrieks. The Maid mindlessly misquotes lines from *Gone With the Wind* ("Ah knows all 'bout birfin' babies, Miz Scarlet. Jus' fetch me dat rusty coat hanga ober dere!"). Twirling across the floor in a daze, the maid cackles and then collapses into a heap. Her tongue lolls from her mouth.

Bubbles walks over to the prostrate Maid and kneels. The Maid pants like a young slut. Her eyes flutter open.

MAID

Nah march upstairs 'n' wash yo' face 'fore ah wear yo' hindpots out wif dis chere spoon o' hot hominy!

Bubbles leaps to her feet and dashes from the kitchen. The Maid laughs long and loud. Dolly in for close shot of Maid's face.

FADE

INT. Subway car—Morning.

SFX: Train's loud locomotive rattle.

Pull back from close shot of the urban-tribal ovals painted on Bubbles' face to medium shot of Bubbles bunched into a ball on the subway train's plastic bench. The train's rock and rumble rattles her bod.

Bubbles is seated between a NURSE and a WINO. The Nurse is fat and black. The Wino is black and babbling.

Sporting a dried-out, high-top Little Richard conk, the Wino is dressed in bits of discarded costuming he discovered in the theater district's trash bins. He wears fungus-covered feather boas, a sequined G-string, fishnet stockings, a gummy, grime-covered gold lamé jacket, and a pair of purple plat-form shoes.

Believing the subway car to be the set for Arsenio Hall's television talk show, the Wino preens for the TV cameras, patting the smears of aqua gel smudged on his high-top conk. He laughs, slaps his thighs, and smokes invisible cigarettes. Feathers and sequins float to the floor.

WINO

I was makin' that big-time money back in 1920. Two-hun'id 'n' fi'ty dollas a week! And do you know why? I was the o-riginal "Little Rascal"! Sunshine Sammy!

Mister Moonpie they used to call me. Yeah! Tha's right! I was before Farina, Stymie, Buckwee—any o' them has-beens!

16

And I was Scrono, too! On the Bowery, with Mugsy and Satch! I even shared billin' with that old-time smecka, Count Dracala! Lemme tell ya, that was no blood he was bangin'! Me 'n' Drac did d'duji! Which was why he was such a freaky muthafucka —Drac flashed *and flipped the fuck out!*

Now I make fi'ty thousand dollars a night! Out in Vegas! With my name in neon high above the strip: "MOKE MOONPIE AND THE MOTOR-CITY MULES!" It's a Motown kinda thang, with Mickey Mouse gloves, big whyte lips, and synchronized dance steps! *We be grinnin' our asses off!*

And I run with the Rat Pack! I'm back-slappin' buddies with Dino, Frank, Sammy, Jerry—and his cripple chirren! I'm Mister *Entertainment* hisself! Why I taught Scatman Crothers ever'thing he knows!

The Nurse, seated on Bubbles' right, looks at the Wino and rolls her eyes in disgust. Tics of annoyance tug at the faces of the other passengers on the subway car. The Wino turns to Bubbles.

WINO

Y'know, we didn't have pussy when I was a boy. That's right. Pussy hadn't been discovered yet. Y'see, pussy was first discovered in 1827 in a cave down in Mississippi by a Massa Johnson. He'd gone out quail huntin' and there it was. *Pussy.* Sittin' right up there in a cave. *Laughin'.*

Bubbles tries to ignore the Wino, but as the Maid's counterspell begins to take effect, exposing Bubbles to her Negrophobic predicament, she grows fearful, her body appearing to wilt smaller and smaller in size.

17

WINO

...I don't know what the hell it is! But let's grease it down and fuck it anyway!

The train stops. Bubbles stares out the window.

Passengers file into the subway car, filling the seats and jamming the aisles. Cattle-crammed bodies sparkle with pungent perspiration. Bubbles wrinkles her nose at the thick Negro smell.

An ALBINO, in kufi skull cap, a floor-length linen robe, billowing bulbed pants, and curved slippers, enters the car carrying a conga drum. He stands by the doors on the left side of the car's far end. The Albino's complexion is the urine hue of unflavored gelatin. His eyes are rabbit pink. His Afro is nicotine yellow.

His palms paddle the skins of the conga drum.

ALBINO

> Listen
> As my snakes
> Slither
> Out of majestic
> African drums.
>
> *Ta dum, ta dum.*
>
> Lost
> Subway children
> In masks of ebony.
> Black wood
> Distorted
> By ivory minds.
>
> *White man*
> Kiss
> My black behind!

An angry voice shouts offscreen.

FIRST VOICE
(o.s.)

Shut up wid dem drums, you funny-lookin' *'Rabian
Nights* nigga! I gots "Wild Eye" poundin' in my
head dis mornin'!!

The Albino paddles his conga skin.

ALBINO

This is no *Arabian Nights* fantasy, brother. This is
the all too real nightmare of *America, the
treacherous!* And I am not a nigger. A nigger exists
only in the blue eyes of the Devil!

My name is Al-Shebop Shabazz Hazred. I'm an
Inner-City Shaman, a Minstrel of Mau Mau
Metaphysics, and a Pop Poet of Oppressed
People's Propaganda. Can you spare a quarter for
Allah?

FIRST VOICE
(o.s.)

Ooooooh please, nigga, *shut up!* My head! *Yo!*
Anybody know what color classification dis'
nigga's complexion qualify for?

SECOND VOICE
(o.s.)

I don't know, but if you rub his 'fro, I bet you a
genie fly out in a puff o' reefa smoke and grant
you three wishes!

The Passengers explode with laughter. In spite of his embarrassment, the Albino continues pounding his conga drum.

DOMESTICS, FACTORY WORKERS, STREET HUSTLERS, JUNKIE
TRANSVESTITES and other SLUM DWELLERS of increasing
strangeness board the subway car and converge on Bubbles
from all sides.

A ring of GHOULISH FACES revolve around the periphery of Bubbles' vision, all with large, bloodshot eyes, bone-pierced nostrils, and clacking, plate-distended lips.

An onrush of fragmented images, evoked in low lit eeriness, stab Bubbles' consciousness in quick succession, congealing into a cubist portrait of urban paranoia. A MINISTER WITH NO FACE, the hollows of his skull covered by a scabbing layer of undulating skin, leans forward and waves his hands before Bubbles in silent malediction. A noisome brood of PALSIED RETARDS, DROOLING MONGOLOIDS, GRINNING PINHEADS, SLITHERING QUADRIPLEGICS, and HUMPBACKED DWARVES shamble through the subway car, squealing and grunting like pigs, clustering around Bubbles in curiosity. They paw her breasts and hair, wheezing a pathetic sound midway between a pant and a whine.

Hyperventilating with terror, Bubbles shuts her eyes in cold horror.

When her eyelids open, Bubbles finds, just inches in front of her nose, a testicle drooping from an open fly, its few strands of pubic hair matted with a crust of dried semen.
Bubbles looks up.

A JUNKIE, stooped in nod, hangs over Bubbles with one hand gripping an overhead strap. His pelvis swings back and forth with the train's rock and rumble. Locomotives and conga thuddings are synchronized to the junkie's pelvic thrusts.

TWO ILL-TEMPERED YOUNG NEGROES stand on either side of the junkie, speaking with fervent intensity. The second Ill-Tempered Young Negro is a cane-tapping sycophant.

FIRST ILL-TEMPERED YOUNG NEGRO
...wall-to-wall whyties. Imagine me, up north, in Maine, with wall-to-wall whyties. Me 'n' dis otha brotha. 'N' he didn't even count. Was one of those upwardly mo'bile niggas of the bougie bougie boogahood.

SECOND ILL-TEMPERED YOUNG NEGRO

An *androided* nigga!

Cane taps twice.

FIRST ILL-TEMPERED YOUNG NEGRO

Right. Manufactured in one of whytie's nigga factories. The original prototype for nigga-baby candy. Popped hot from a monster mold.

SECOND ILL-TEMPERED YOUNG NEGRO

A *klingon* nigga!

Cane taps twice.

FIRST ILL-TEMPERED YOUNG NEGRO

A klingon nigga. The Coon From Planet X. Spoke an alien tongue. Jus' me 'n' dis out-o'-tune buffoon 'mongst wall-to-wall whyties. As a gen-u-wine jitta buggin' jigaboo, dem hunkies made it a point t'check me out! Ofay bitches was always accidentally-on-purpose bumpin' dey titties in my face 'n' rubbin' my kinks, talkin' 'bout, *"It do feel like a Brillo pad!"* In the mornin', when I be takin' my shower, I was pullin' fistfuls o' blond pussy hair out o' my crotch!

First Ill-Tempered Young Negro shakes his knees and grabs his penis.

FIRST ILL-TEMPERED YOUNG NEGRO

Brutha, *I was gunnin'!*

SECOND ILL-TEMPERED YOUNG NEGRO

Gunnin' the Great White Bitch!

Cane taps twice.

21

FIRST ILL-TEMPERED YOUNG NEGRO

Gunnin' the Great White Bitch! I swore the total annihilation of the entire whyte race and anything left over with the faintest trace of that demon hunkie scent—*for the bitch drove me mad!*

Was nuthin' a nigga could relate to. A world without James Brown forty-fives!

SECOND ILL-TEMPERED YOUNG NEGRO

No James Brown forty-fives!

Cane taps twice.

FIRST ILL-TEMPERED YOUNG NEGRO

No *Jet* magazines!

SECOND ILL-TEMPERED YOUNG NEGRO

No Jet magazines!

Cane taps twice.

FIRST ILL-TEMPERED YOUNG NEGRO

No greasy collard greens!

SECOND ILL-TEMPERED YOUNG NEGRO

No greasy collard greens!

Cane taps twice.

The Two Ill-Tempered Young Negroes glower at Bubbles with reddened coke-glazed eyes. Dolly in for close shot of Bubbles' face.

FIRST ILL-TEMPERED YOUNG NEGRO
(o.s.)

Jus' my black ass an' a Afro pick!

Second Ill-Tempered Young Negro taps cane twice. Echo taps and fade to blacks.

INT. Donald Goines Senior High—Classroom—Day

Fade up on the punkadelic blond dreads of a black-skinned GIRL. Slowly pan left to right, overlap dissolve, and pan right to left across the faces of the other STUDENTS seated in the classroom, each face a frightening caricature of the grotesque.

BUBBLES

(v.o.)

My high school was overridden with niggas. Not the slow-witted, slow-shufflin', eyeball-rollin', flapjack-flippin' niggas in the brownstones off Central Park West. Or the upwardly mobile, paper-bag-colored Klingon niggas of the bougie boogahood. But nigger niggas—*the nightmarish kind!*

Mindless angel-dusted darkies slobbering insane single syllables, flicking switchblades and flashing straightrazors. Hip-Hoppity jungle bunnies in brightly colored clothes, carrying large, loud radios we white wits call "Spadios," who drank bubbling purple carbonates and ate fried pork rinds and bag after bag of dehydrated potato slices caked with orange dust. Crotch-clawin' niggas who talked *Deputy Dawg* and shot dope. Saucer-lipped ragoons who called me the "Ozark Mountain She-Devil" and asked to feel my lunch money. Percussive porch monkeys who fart with their faces to a heavy-metal beat.

These were the kind of niggas my daddy warned me about. The kind of niggas my daddy said would whisk me off to the Isle of Unrestrained Negroes far, far away, and turn me into a coal-black pickaninny with a nappy ribbon top and white button eyes if I wasn't a good girl and didn't do as daddy said.

At the close of the Ku Klux Cartoon Coon Show in the classroom, stop on Bubbles seated at her desk.

SFX: Hammer of electric school bell.

Bubbles stands up from her desk. Instantly, she's swept into the rush of students jostling their way through the door. As she wrestles against the press of bodies, a finger swiftly slides between the cheeks of her behind. Bubbles recoils, and her eyebrows rise in surprise.

BUBBLES

Leaping lizards!

INT: Donald Goines Senior High—Corridor—Day

The corridor's physical structure combines the utilitarian interiors of a public school building with the depressed exteriors of a ghetto slum. The mood is chaotic circus funk.

Tin whistles toot. Bass lines wa-wa. And students bark woof-woof-woof.

At the rear of the seemingly ceilingless corridor is a gun tower, enclosed by barbed wire, a cyclone fence, and a pack of slavering Doberman pinschers. Inside the gun tower, a GUNNER sits behind a brace of machine guns. The sign of the gun tower reads in punctured block letters:

The corridor's column of lockers is a dazzle of wildstyle designs: multicolored sprays of Vaughn Bodé nymphs entangled inside gnarled, Escheresque girders who fellate duck-billed home boys with floating thought balloons of musical notations and fried chicken parts above their heads. Huge posters of Marcus Garvey, Malcolm X, and Bob Marley are wheat-pasted all along the hall. Black, red, and green sewer steam billows from a manhole cover sunk into the floor. The front end of a car with a drinking fountain built into its toothy chrome grill projects from a wall. Iron grates are pulled across the doors. Sections of the wall are crumbling, and bricks are strewn about the floor. Neon BAR, PAWN SHOP, JESUS SAVES, and HOT PORK CHOPS AND COLD BEER signs flash in distracting sequence.

Throngs of students congest the corridor smoking resinous Rasta spliffs; inhaling in brown paper bags sticky with airplane glue; snorting smack from tiny, waxed-paper sacks; drinking pints of Wild Irish Rose; sucking tubes of crack; fighting with razors; firing pistols; dry humping each other against lockers; hawking stolen goods; miscarrying half-formed fetuses; singing gospel; and wailing the blues.

A 200-pound BLACK MUSLIM, in a well-tailored suit and maroon bow tie, stands, like a ringmaster, in the center of the corridor's confusion, with a bundle of newspapers under his arm. He holds up a copy of *Muhammad Speaks,* with a "Whitie the Devil" cartoon on its front cover: A horned Uncle Sam stabs a pious black minister in the ass with the prongs of a flaming trident. The cartoon is captioned, "Amerikkka is *hell,* nigger!"

200-POUND BLACK MUSLIM

Paper, brutha? Don'cho' wan' a paper?
Whatsamatta? Whyte man stole y'mind 'n' put a
hole in yo' soul? C'mon, brutha—*do fo' sef! Ah buys
a bundle ever' week! Ah jus' luz doze cartoons! D'way*

dey be makin' d'whyte man look lak d'debil 'n' shit—
y'know, wid dem horns, dat tail, 'n' dem freakie feets—
ah be laffin' 'til my ass shake!

The Muslim bursts into laughter, his rotund ass shaking like a bowl of Jell-O.

Bottles, bricks, and Afro picks whiz past Bubbles' head as she wanders through an assemblage of robotic POPLOCKERS. A HUMAN DRUM MACHINE belches to the beat.

200-POUND BLACK MUSLIM

Or how 'bout some Shabazz Bean Pie, brutha? It be good fo' stabilizin' yo' blacktitude. Did you know, affa eatin' a slice o' bean pie, some bruthas have been known to fart all four sides of Brutha Miles' *Bitches Brew* out dey butts? The stench be so foul and unholy, the Honorable Elijah Muhammad hisself awakes wide-eyed in his coffin!

The Gunner fires a spray of bullets into the crew of POPPERS, LOCKERS, and HEAD-SPINNERS. Blood spurts. Eyeballs fly. Heads explode. Jaws shatter. Intestines dangle. All in disgusting *Dawn of the Dead* detail.

SFX: Machine-gun fire from the soundtrack of the 1974 SLA shoot-out news footage.

The 200-pound Black Muslim is riddled with bullets from head to toe. Blood oozes from his wounds and down his suit. Half his face is ripped away. With ribbons of flesh flapping against exposed bone, the Muslim quakes with laughter. He then falls face forward to the floor. And farts. Loudly. The seat of his pants flutters in flatulent winds. A brown nuclear cloud hangs over him. He utters—

200-POUND BLACK MUSLIM

...*bean* pie, brutha.

—and dies.

27

Unharmed, unbloodied, and, apparently, invulnerable, the oblivious Bubbles doesn't even notice. Three grunting, pig-snouted POLICE OFFICERS blackjack a black-bereted student with a "RESURRECT HUEY!" button pinned to the lapel of his black leather jacket. A gush of his brain pulp flies by. Bubbles doesn't notice this either.

A CHICKEN leaps from behind and lands on her shoulder. She cringes. The chicken squawks and drops to the floor. A lanky TEEN with a protruding Adam's apple steps around Bubbles, following the chicken. He leans low to the floor with his hands shoved in his pockets, his elbows crooked and flapping. He has one eye open and the other eye closed.

SFX: Hard, metallic whir.

Bubbles' ears perk to attention. The whir builds to a grating metal-grinding pitch. The sound sets Bubbles' teeth on edge.

A ROLLER DERBY QUEEN skates behind Bubbles, circling around and around. On the front of the Roller Queen's black, red, and green jersey, embroidered around a soft-scuplture relief of Aunt Jemima's face in a waxing crescent moon, are the words:

AUNT JEMIMA'S FLAPJACK NINJA-KILLERS FROM HELL

A pair of crossed gold spatulas tattoo a breast thrusting through the jersey's elastic opening. The Ninja Queen grins. Her nipple stiffens. The Ninja Queen rolls around and around. She appears and disappears. Her wheels slow to a stop. She and Bubbles stand nose to nose.

The Ninja Queen spits.

The worm of spit doesn't squirm down Bubbles' cheek. It *sticks*.

The Ninja Queen turns and rolls away. Bubbles stands in the corridor with the clot of mucus stuck to her cheek, fumbling for a tissue in her pockets. Finding none, she tries to finger it from her face. As she stares in disgust at the viscid slime on her fingertip, a firecracker snaps above her head.

Bubbles walks through a hail of bottles, bricks, and more Afro picks to a door marked "GIRLS." The letters on the door have been slashed with a pen knife and the word "HOZE" has been carved in its place. She opens the door and walks in.

INT. Donald Goines Senior High—Girls' lavatory—Day.

EIGHT FLAPJACK NINJA QUEENS—outfitted in shoulder and knee pads, roller skates, and one-breast jerseys—slouch against the back wall. Joints are passed and smoked.

FLAPJACK 0

...*an apple in a baby's fist, my ass!* It look more like a gross green grub wif a marble in its mouf! I mean you shoulda *heard* dis nigga! He say "Ah knows d'ham hocks mus' be hot, 'cause d'grits be bubblin' in d'pot!" Da nigga's eyes roll back in his head, his lashes start to flappin', an' da nigga screamed, "Good Gawd, girl! D'greens is greasy now!" An' I thought, "Would you listen to dis no-dick country fool!"

FLAPJACK 00

Den why you give him some den?

FLAPJACK 0

Well, girl, you know how it—

As Bubbles walks into the lavatory, the Ninja Queens turn and greet her with icy stares. Bubbles pauses with her back pressed against the door.

Ignoring them, Bubbles walks to the row of porcelain sinks lining the right wall. Above the sinks, a horizontal mirror extends from one end of the wall to the other. In the mirror, she examines the stiff blob stuck to her silver disks.

FLAPJACK 25
I see Miss Ann's come to use the can!

Bubbles watches the Ninja Queens' reflection in the mirror.

FLAPJACK 6
She act like she don't shit 'cause she can't find paper soft enough to wipe her ass with.

FLAPJACK 0
I wonder if she know how?

FLAPJACK 6
Miss Ann—you know how to *shit?*

Bubbles' mouth is a jittering black line. Watching the Ninja Queens' reflection in the mirror, she cautiously reaches inside her jacket for the straight razor. Suddenly realizing this could prove quite fatal, especially to herself, she lets the razor slide back.

FLAPJACK 25
Looks like this girl could use a little toilet trainin'.

FLAPJACK 42
Yeah! Funky entertainment—*steamin' hot!*

FLAPJACK 25
Drag her hunkie ass over here and let's get on with it!

The Ninja Queens separate into two groups. Four skate to the middle of the lavatory. The remainder roll to the row of sinks.

Flapjack 13 rolls to Bubbles and grabs her by the braids, yanking her around. Bubbles shoves her across the floor. Rolling backward, Flapjack 13 falls on her ass.

BUBBLES

Get your filthy monkey paws off of me!

Flapjack 13 heaves herself off the floor with a gleeful bloodlust in her eyes.

FLAPJACK 13

Miss Ann wants to jump baad! G'on widja pale, assless self, Miss Ann. *Jump!*

With a deft Ali shuffle on her roller skates, Flapjack 13 spins her fists, giving Bubbles a push. Bubbles pushes back.

BUBBLES

I said *keep your fucking monkey paws off of me!*

Flapjack 13 stops. Frowns. *Pouts.*

FLAPJACK 13

Who you callin' "monkey," hunkie?

BUBBLES

Who you callin' "hunkie," monkey?

FLAPJACK 13

You! BITCH!

Grinning, Bubbles squints in defiance. She boldly walks up to Flapjack 13. The two girls stand tit to tit.

Felch me.

The Ninja Queens goad them on in the background.

FLAPJACK NINJA QUEENS
(o.s.)

Whoooo-ooooo! That's nasty! Tonja, you gon' take that offa whyte girl?!

Flapjack 13's eyebrow cocks in confusion.

FLAPJACK 13

What "'felchin'"?

BUBBLES

A verb! Y'dumb, corn-bread-crunchin' *coon!*

The remark churns fears, frustrations, and animosities that Flapjack 13 cannot name nor Bubbles understand. She slaps Bubbles across the face, streaking her hand with the clot of snot. The rope of snot finally drops.

FLAPJACK 13

Corn bread *good!* Tonja like corn bread! And pig tails, *too!* Like dat funky singa say, It make Tonja happy!

FLAPJACK 25
(o.s.)

You talk about Tonja's corn bread and pigtails, it's just like you talkin' about Tonja *mama!*

FLAPJACK 13

Don't you talk about my mama!

Bubbles' eyes are round with disbelief. She backs away.

Oh, shit! This steroid-swollen *he-bitch* is about to go berserk! (Help!)

Flapjack 13 swings her arms in blind fury, charges like an angry bull, and stumbles over her roller skates. She hits the floor.

FLAPJACK 13

Umph!

As she gets up, Bubbles jumps on her back and rides her like a rodeo bronco-buster.

The gang of Ninja Queens tosses lit matches at Bubbles as she lurches on the enraged Flapjack 13's padded shoulders.

FLAPJACK NINJA QUEENS

Kill that bitch! Kick the whyte out her ass!
Where's the lighter fluid? Let's set that bitch on
fire!

Flapjack 13's back bucks up and down. Bubbles pulls her hair, gouges her eyes, and bites her nose. Choking her in a headlock, Bubbles leans over and bites her exposed black breast.

BUBBLES

Chomp!

FLAPJACK 13
(screaming)

D'biddie bit m'tittie!

Flapjack 13 swings her shoulders back and forth like a set of tavern doors. As she attempts to flip Bubbles to the floor, jerking her back in a downward swoop, Flapjack 13 falls to the floor herself. Bubbles lands in a tangle on top of her, scissoring the Ninja Queen's head between her thighs. The Ninja Queen bites Bubbles in the V of her Spandex crotch. Blond hairs sprout from the tear.

In disgust, Flapjack 25 shoves Bubbles off of Flapjack 13. She points to the middle of the floor.

> **FLAPJACK 25**
> *(o.s.)*
>
> Enough of this bullshit. Drag her hunkie ass over there.

Six Ninja Queens drag Bubbles across the tiles by the braids of her hair. Flapjack 25 watches with her fists propped on her hips. Flapjack 13 whimpers in a corner, massaging her bruised breast. The Ninja Queens form a half circle around Bubbles. Switchblades are flicked in a clockwise direction.

Click! Click! Click!

> **FLAPJACK 25**
> *(o.s.)*
>
> *Stand up!*

Bubbles stands.

> **FLAPJACK 25**
> *(o.s.)*
>
> Now *piss*, bitch!!

The Ninja Queens prod Bubbles with the points of their blades. Dewlike gold drops glisten on the blond shoots of her pubic hair. And trickle down her leg.

Bubbles sinks into the widening yellow puddle on the floor. Tears bead on her ovals of silver greasepaint. Medium shot of Bubbles folded in a fetal ball on the floor with a row of muscular brown legs behind her.

FLAPJACK 19
(o.s.)

What is that devilish mess caked on her face?

FLAPJACK 54
(o.s.)

Magically converging uteri equalizing her aura's balance of negative and positive energies.

FLAPJACK 19
(o.s.)

Why she do that?

FLAPJACK 54
(o.s.)

What else is a whyte girl to do in a school full of jigaboos?

FADE

INT. Brownstone—Hall—Late Afternoon.

SFX: Tumblers clicking in door lock.

Bubbles enters the brownstone's darkened hallway, closing the door behind her. With a languid sweep of her hand, she flips the switch on the wall to the right of the door, illuminating the hall with a weak overhead bulb. The brownstone is dark and quiet, and its furnishings are veiled in still shadows. Its sibilant hush lulls her into sleepy lethargy. She slumps against the door.

Blood entwined with strings of saliva drool off her lumped lower lip. Mucus and tears stain her cheeks in a smear of silver rivulets.

Finally, Bubbles treads the length of the hallway's corridor with all the exhausted vitality of a zombie toiling in the Haitian cane fields, her keys jingling between pinched fingers.

SFX: The jingle of door keys. The clump of boots on the carpet.

She stops at the staircase facing the living room and clicks the light switch at the foot of the stairs. Dazed, she climbs the stairs with plodding Frankenstein footfalls. At the head of the stairs, she stares down the corridor of the second-floor landing. A drip splashes in the distance, muted.

Bubbles walks in the direction of the persistent *drip, drip, drip* with uneasy caution. She stops at her bedroom's half-open door, hearing a squish beneath her boot. She looks down.

Diluted blood has seeped into the carpet. Her neck is splashed.

She looks up. Blanketed in frost, a frozen chicken thaws at the end of a wire nailed to the top of the door frame. Close-up of blood dripping from the chicken's ass end.

Bubbles is splashed with blood. It dribbles across her nose and into her ear, cutting strange designs in the silver smear. Pull back from close shot of Bubbles' face dotted with beads of blood and silver.

CUT TO:

INT. Brownstone—Bathroom—Late afternoon.

Medium shot of Bubbles in a bathroom fogged with steam. She lounges in a tub heaped with suds, an arm and a leg hanging over the side. A joint smolders between her fingertips.

Bubbles lifts the joint to her swollen mouth. Stoned and drowsy, she strains to keep her eyes open. She nods and drops the joint into the bathwater. Her eyes open and narrow, rolling in suspicion. Finally, she falls asleep.

Dolly in to steam wafting around her head and blur to dissolve.

INT. White Womb Theater.

The Womb Theater's stage is curtained with the membranes of dried afterbirth. Its white gauze-covered walls curve like the inside of an eggshell. Its floor is flat and tiled with a high-polish white plastic.

Bubbles, onstage, is trapped inside a bank of tapiocalike gel with large, luminous worms squirming inside its translucent sacs. The gel sticks to the contours of her body like a weird uncontrolled fungus. It encases her neck, the back of her head, her arms, ankles, and rib cage. Her knees are propped up, bent, and spread. Her blond valentine mons gleams in the footlights.

Sheathed in a white silk glove, a HAND reaches between her thighs and withdraws a WHITE RABBIT. In a white, short-coated tuxedo, a WITCH DOCTOR holds the rabbit in the air with his hand balled around its ears. He grins.

SFX: Hand-pounding, foot-stomping, whistles, and cheers.

The Witch Doctor crouches over Bubbles. His skin is coal black. His eyes are yoke yellow and the size of duck eggs. The corners of his red, rubbery mouth bubble with greenish foam. Flies feed off the drool hanging from his filed yellow teeth. His wiry hair spits straight into the air.

With her eyes bulging in terror, Bubbles turns away and looks into the audience—

JACK JOHNSON in pugilist pose, wearing boxing trunks and gloves; MARCUS GARVEY and HIS FOLLOWERS in paramilitary dress; STEPIN FETCHIT sharing a spliff with BOB MARLEY; DUKE ELLINGTON with GEORGE CLINTON and his P-FUNK MOB; SONNY LISTON; ROSA PARKS; BILL "BOJANGLES" ROBINSON; an empty lunch counter; the JACKSON 5; ADAM CLAYTON POWELL, JR.; BESSIE SMITH; JAMES BALDWIN; BOBO BRAZIL; ELDRIDGE CLEAVER; SHIRLEY TEMPLE in pickaninny blackface; CHARLIE "YARDBIRD" PARKER; AUNT JEMIMA; HATTIE MCDANIEL; BUTTERFLY MCQUEEN; LOUISE BEAVERS; LITTLE STEVIE WONDER; BIG STEVIE WONDER; STOKELY CARMICHAEL; MIRIAM MAKEBA; MUHAMMAD ALI; CASSIUS CLAY; NINA SIMONE; MOMS MABLEY; ANGELFOOD MCSPADE; BOBBY SEALE; JAMES BROWN; ZOMBEEZI; PRINCE RANDIAN "THE CATERPILLAR MAN"; AMIRI BARAKA; LEROI JONES; WILLIE BEST; FATHER DIVINE; WILLIE MAYS; MA RAINEY; GENERAL BENJAMIN O. DAVIS; the nine SCOTTSBORO BOYS; HOWLIN' WOLF; DIZZY GILLESPIE; the GOLD DUST TWINS; BUCK and BUBBLES; RAY CHARLES; MARIE LAVEAU; RUDY RAY MOORE; LOUIS ARMSTRONG with the KING OLIVER CREOLE JAZZ BAND; RICHARD PRYOR; DONALD GOINES; JOE LOUIS; AMOS, ANDY, the KING FISH, and NICK O'DEMUS as "LIGHTNIN'"; ANGELA DAVIS; the NEW ORLEANS ZULU KREWE; EMMETT TILL; CAB CALLOWAY; MISSISSIPPI JOHN HURT; ELIJAH MUHAMMAD; UNCLE REMUS; PAUL ROBESON; REDD FOXX; HUEY LEDBETTER; FLAMBEAU TORCHBEARERS; CLARENCE MUSE; MALCOLM X; JIMMY "J.J." WALKER; UNCLE BEN; MELVIN VAN PEEBLES; LOUIS FARRAKHAN; FARINA; PEETIE WHEATSTRAW; MANTAN MORELAND; SUGAR RAY ROBINSON; JIMMIE LUNCEFORD; DR. JOHN; THOMAS "FATS" WALLER; the LAST POETS; LITTLE RICHARD; OSCAR MICHEAUX; SAMMY DAVIS, JR.; BILL COSBY; OSSIE DAVIS; RUBY DEE; LOUIS JORDAN; EDDIE MURPHY; PROFESSOR GRIFF; ETHEL MOSES; MATTHEW "STYMIE" BEARD; LOTHAR; H. RAP BROWN; PRINCE; EDDIE "ROCHESTER" ANDERSON; PHAROAH SANDERS; BOSCO and his grandma's cookies; SIDNEY POITIER; ICEBERG SLIM; HUEY NEWTON; ARCHIE SHEPP; BUCKWEE; and, of course, MARTIN LUTHER KING, JR., with blood-stained bullet holes in his shirt. The audience holds up a large, unfurled banner. It reads:

WELCOME TO THE APOLLO

SFX: Loud cheering and applause.

The Witch Doctor pulls another rabbit from between Bubbles' legs. She twitches with convulsions. Her pores pop with sweat. Her belly heaves in and out. Her vulva sputters.

SFX: Hot, heavy panting.

Shreds of membrane dangle from the ceiling. The Witch Doctor cackles. The audience cheers. HUNDREDS OF WHITE RABBITS huddle onstage. Thousands of pink eyes stare from a white field of fur.

Darkness wafts in. Pink shifts to red.

SFX: Fade panting and bring up soft night sounds—a breeze rustling through the trees' leaves, the whir and chirp of crickets. Cross-fade to:

EXT. Forest—Night.

A multitude of small red eyes dot the darkness. The illumination of the moon outlines the shapes of rocks and trees.

Pull back to long shot and reveal black-furred rabbits peering from the brush. Continue pulling back to Extreme Long Shot and reveal the tops of trees with the rabbits receding into the background underneath.

Barefoot in bone anklets and leopardskin bikini, with a leather pouch hanging off her hip, Bubbles stands on the crest of a hill, her figure silhouetted against the moon, holding a rice-paper parasol.

Bubbles looks to her left, then to her right, and strolls down the hill. Smooth white stones glitter in her path.

Dragonflies hover. Fireflies blink.

She pauses at a cluster of large, luminous mushrooms sprouting along the border of the path. Kneeling, she stuffs her pouch with the bright, bulbous caps.

Still red eyes without iris or pupil watch.

Munching a spotted mushroom, Bubbles resumes her stroll. Wind rustles through the leaves of the trees and carries the ghostly whispers of a flute. She stops. Her pupils contract to pinpoints.

With woolly legs and sable skin, a cleft-hooved SATYR squats on a boulder nestled under the branches of a willow tree. His head is bald and hornless, with large, sharply pointed ears. His eyes burn bright as coals. A large curved penis bounces between his thighs. The Satyr blows on a wooden flute with a merry leer. Watchful rabbits huddle in the shade.

As the Satyr's penis pulses to his flute's eerie song, Bubbles shivers with her lips aquiver and bounces on the balls of her toes. She reaches for the folds of her vulva, fingers the bead of her clit, and bites her lower lip. Long, lively fingers skip skillfully along the flute holes.

Bubbles is transfixed by the Satyr's massive dick. The music and her tension build to a climactic pitch. Spasmodic with fluids, she swoons and pops, her eyes shifting in color from pale green to ice silver and back again.

The Satyr leaps from the boulder with his penis pounding in the air. He dances rings around Bubbles, wagging his penis just beyond her grasp. Her eyes follow the penis as the Satyr skips away.

Trailed by the clutch of rabbits, Bubbles follows. She grabs for the penis. It isn't there. She catches air. The Satyr laughs as his penis bobs away. Bubbles grabs again, and misses, stumbling over rabbits underfoot.

As the rabbits hop away, Bubbles lifts her head and finds her rice-paper parasol in a splintered pile at the Satyr's hooves.

The Satyr smiles his leering smile. And slowly fades away.

His face fades by degrees. Leafless trees with gnarled limbs and thousands of twisting black branches mask a cold, foreboding moon with a fan of arteries visible through his fading features. His face fades until his eyes are two glowing embers, fades until only his music is heard in the breeze rustling the trees' leaves.

Silence.

The flute falls to earth and rolls into the huddle of rabbits. Bubbles heaves off the ground, picking through the shreds of colored paper and shards of broken bamboo. She cocks her ear and listens. Howls and gutteral growls.

Bubbles turns. In varying stages of transformation, the rabbits are turning into dogs. Or more precisely—*Doberman pinschers*. Some die in the agonizing process.

Bubbles spins around in wild panic. Tarred lynching victims hang from the trees. Corpses protrude from the ground in grotesque poses. A WOMAN with her stomach slashed drags a rotted fetus on the end of an uncoiled umbilical cord. A face in the clay. An arm. A severed hand. The SHADOWS OF HOODED MEN prowl amid the woods' other shadows.

Looking back at the mutating rabbit pack, Bubbles runs. MUTANT DOGS with long floppy ears and fluffy tails snarl and snap at her heels. Castrated genitalia litter the ground.

EXT. Cemetery—Night.

Bubbles runs through the open gate of a cemetery enclosed by a rusted wrought-iron fence. Inside, she tumbles over a toppled stone. Clenched in solidarity salute, a BLACK FIST bursts through the dirt, clamping its fingers around Bubbles' ankle.

Hot eyes and slavering fangs in swirling lime-colored mists.

The Mutants bound across the barren burial ground in grainy, supernatural slo-mo.

Bubbles tugs against the Black Fist's grip, looking back at the approaching Mutant Pack. A Mutant leaps. And a blur of eyes, teeth, and saliva close around Bubbles' throat. The FIST fades to bright, blood-red bathwater.

INT. Brownstone—Bathroom—Evening.

Bubbles gasps awake. The fist fades in bright, blood-red bathwater. The suds in the tub are a flat pink froth. A soggy joint floats in the water's rippling rings.

                    BUBBLES
    Christ, my period...!

INT. Brownstone—Bedroom—Evening.

Close-up of an unwavering candle flame.

Pull back and reveal the surface of a mirror with the candle placed in front of it. The mirror, streaked with menstrual blood in the shape of a figure eight, shows a labyrinth of reflections cast by the other mirrors in the room, all ritually arranged with incense and lit candles. The mirror shows, too, Bubbles, nude, on her four-poster mahogany bed, clipping the hair between her thighs with a pair of manicure scissors.

The candle flames flicker with sudden violence, and a flurry of air whisks the room.

The camera follows this surge of movement—which emits a sound, imperceptible to Bubbles's ears, like notes cackled through a soprano saxophone—and stops on a shard of broken mirror, dusted with chips of cocaine and flakes of tobacco, lying on the nightstand by the bed. The grains of cocaine begin to move, lining up in formation like iron filings guided by a magnetic wand, and disappear. The flurry of air scurries away in a trail of musical giddiness.

BUBBLES
(v.o.)

Sometimes I feel like the little girl in *Night of the Living Dead.*

On the wall above Bubbles' bed, another mirror reflects her image at many angles and repeats it into infinity. In front of the mirror, a pocket of air pressure pops and spurts a viscid, aqua ooze, which evaporates in a burble of giggles.

44

The dead devour the living, dragging ragged
flesh through dirt, sucking down ropes of
intestines like so much pasta.

Dolly in to the mirror's maze of multiple images, all candle
flames and flesh, and dissolve to a close-up of Bubbles' cunt.

BUBBLES

(v.o.)

Blood rings the child's mouth. She kneels by her
father's corpse—gnawing on her *dear, dead, daddy's*
arm. She murders her mother with a garden
trowel.

Scissors pare her heart-shaped wreath of pubic hair. Tilt up
the moist pout of her vulva, over her belly's bed of fine down
to the slit of her navel, and continue to the V of her cleavage.

Angle on the contours of her full, sloping breasts and pan
across her swollen, rose-colored areolas.

BUBBLES

(v.o.)

Why do I want to eat my parents?

Dolly 180 degrees to her back. Tilt up to an over-the-
shoulder shot of her face in the glass. And the ellipses of
menstrual blood circling her eyes.

BUBBLES

(v.o.)

To puke them up, of course!

Dolly in to mirror and reverse angle.

Bubbles blows a stream of coca smoke through her nostrils. The swell of smoke curls with the slow slither of a drugged serpent around her dilated and menses-masked eyes. She crushes the head of her joint in the nightstand's ashtray and stretches her arms in the air.

Arching her back, she rolls her head about her neck, flexing splayed fingers. Her tongue lolls comfortably from her mouth.

Bubbles zazens in the radiance of candlelight and its reflections.

Suddenly, the door swings open and bangs against the wall. The candles are blown out in unison. All the mirrors fall.

The Maid's imposing bulk fills the open door, her shadow looming large and dark across the floor. The chicken, nailed to the top of the door frame, revolves above her head. Droplets of blood splash her scalp and spill down her face. She clutches a pair of sewing shears in her right fist.

MAID

Ah jus' bets you wonnerin' what ah intends on doin' wif dis big ol' pair of cuttin' shairs—!

The Maid whips her left arm from behind her back and reveals a squeeze tube in her fist.

MAID

—'n dis cheer tube o' K-Y!

She lumbers toward Bubbles with slow, thudding footfalls. The floorboards crack with every step.

MAID

First, ah's gwine cut d'locks off'n y'haid!

Bubbles crab-scuttles on her back to the upper left-hand corner of her bed.

46

*Den ah's gwine grine hembane 'n' bellydonna berries wif
some o' dat good rasta reefa dem nappy-haided niggas
sell down at d'candy sto' 'n' mix it up wif d'K-Y!*

Bubbles sprawls against the back wall holding a tangle of
sheets to her breasts. The Maid stands at the edge of the bed,
shoving the sewing shears and tube of K-Y into her apron's
front pockets. Her eyes and teeth gleam in the dark.

MAID

*Den ah's gwine glop d'K-Y Juju jelly-jam down 'round
y'titties 'n' up 'twixt y'ass—arubbin' 'n' apokin' till it
melts into y'pores 'n' gits down into y'blood! 'N' whilst yo'
ass be doin' d'freakie-deekie on d'bellydonna, ah'mo roll
d'res' o' dat rasta reefa into a big spliff, slap on some
zootin' Calloway sides, 'n' blow dat spliff lak ah's a
howg-ridin' hophead in Harlem! Hah!*

The Maid lunges, grabs Bubbles by the braids, and winds
them around her wrist. Bubbles is a flurry of legs and fists.
The Maid yanks at the roots of Bubbles' hair. Bubbles is
paralyzed with pain and acute despair. The Maid drags her
off the bed, and Bubbles hits the floor.

Caught by her ankles, Bubbles gropes about, her fingers
finding the collar of the black leather jacket lying beneath
the bed.

CUT TO:

Long shot, from under bed, of Bubbles, with the collar of her
jacket bunched in the ball of her fist. She is then dragged by
the Maid through lumps of melted candle wax and shattered
mirror glass, out of the bedroom, and along the hall.

As Bubbles recedes into the background, reverse angle and
dolly in for close shot of the bed's rear-left leg.

Aqua ooze spurts in a twitter of giggles and evaporates, and translucent outlines slowly take shape in a shimmer of gold and cocoa hues. A tiny upright soprano saxophone stands on its mouth by the bed's leg. A nude, coal-skinned IMP with sharp, crescent features convulsed in laughter sits by the saxophone, jacking off. His pelvis bounces under his tiny fist.

Fade to:

INT. Brownstone—Attic—Night.

In close-up, track the objects arranged in the attic's rotted wood floor: Melted Barbie dolls in mangled poses—arms, legs contorted in puddles of hardened plastic; heads welded to hands; pins piercing quadriplegic torsos of muted gender—black skull candles bleeding beads of red wax; maggots writhing inside the mouth of a severed dog's head; cryptic Afro-pictograms in metallic red marker on a black statuette of Marilyn Monroe; flour and ash in swirling designs; jars filled with eyeballs, human hearts, fully formed fetuses, and inverted crosses floating in murky green fluids on the lower shelves of a multitiered alter; censors smoking with nasty odors; and the tail of a RAT receding into a hole.

SFX: Synthetic, computerized drum rhythms beat stadium-loud through a boom box's huge dual speakers.

The door in the attic's floor squeals open with a phlegmatic peal. The Maid rumbles through like a monstrous black beetle, dragging Bubbles behind her—*bump! bump! bump!*

MAID

If papa doc kin bring 'bout d'sassination ob d'res'dent ob d'Nited States wif his juju*, ah kin cer'inly drive a young whyte gal crazy wif mine! Kee! Kee! Kee!

---

*Voodoo terrorists take note.

48

The Maid locks Bubbles' wrists into a pair of handcuffs connected to a chain-and-pulley system suspended from the ceiling. She heaves Bubbles off the floor, grunting with each tug on the pulley's rope.

Bubbles dangles rag-doll dumb. Her teeth chatter. The muscles of her jaw constrict in a cold mix of cocaine and terror.

The Maid drops the handcuffs' key into her apron's front pocket and withdraws the pair of sewing shears, brandishing them in Bubbles' face.

MAID

So you don't kno' wha' choo do wifout yo' mane o' Goldi-tale fairy-locks, huh? Hah! Well, weeze jus' gwine hafta see 'bout dat, won't we?

The Maid snips a lock of Bubbles' hair and steps back with her fist on her hip.

MAID

How 'bout a "hep" hunkie doo-doo cut, lak dat crowd o'rich junkies wear downtown, wif d'ziggity zags 'n' criss-crosses cut all into dey haids! Or maybe you'd like a conservative boll-dagga buzz cut? Or would you r'fer som'n wil' 'n' stylus but 'spec'fully tasteful—lak you jus' come back fum radiation treatment fo' terminus cancer!

SFX: The hiss of slow and oppressed breathing.

A mustache of sweat beads on the Maid's upper lip. Her mouth trembles into an agitated smile. She lifts her hand to delicately caress Bubbles' bruised and swollen face. Instead, she grabs Bubbles by her two braids and yanks her hair at the roots, whispering—

When ah tetch you lak dis', wif yo' hair balled in
m'fist, it sets my grits to boil *an' bubbles down
m'leg*!

The boom blaster blares a frenetically energetic and wholly
schizophrenic audio collage of fifties sci-fi and kung-fu
movie soundtracks integrated into a studio remix of James
Brown's "Cold Sweat." This fuels the frenzy of the Maid's
snipping shears. A blizzard of blond falls to the floor and
glitters in the skull-candle's light.

Save for two tufts of hair arcing over her right ear and
another swaying over her brow, Bubbles is left nicked,
bleeding, and bald.

The Maid drops her shears. She falls to her knees and
unloads the contents of her apron's front pockets on the
floor: mortar, pestle, K-Y tube, a branch of belladonna,
henbane, and a compressed square of marijuana buds. White
noise issues from the boom box's speakers.

MAID

Kee! Kee! Kee!

The Maid plucks berries from the belladonna branch, crumbles henbane in her fist, and unravels buds from the reefer
square.

MAID

*Dis blend made me mighty pop'lar in d'sixties when ah
was dealin' to d'hippies!*

She tosses the herbs into the mortar's bowl and grinds them
down with her pestle.

Ah was o' mess back den! M'name was "Moonpie" 'n' ah wore high-warda bell-bottoms dat hung an inch ova m'ankles 'n' was too tight fo' m'ass! D'waist stopped three-quarters up 'n' m'ass fell in lumps ova d'top! You could see crack fo' days! Kee! Kee! Kee!

A worm of ooze is squeezed from the K-Y tube. And the concoction glows a ghastly green. The Maid dips her hands into the bowl. Then her fingers slide into the folds of Bubbles' cunt.

The Maid puts her menses-tipped fingers in her mouth. Her fevered grin spreads like buckwheat batter plopped into a hot buttered skillet.

The Maid stands, shrieks, and rattles her breasts in a quiversome trance dance—barking like a dog, mewling like a cat, and hissing like a snake. She smears the gel on Bubbles' body with lascivious care.

Bubbles twists, turns, and gyrates in sweaty serpentine squiggles. The boom blaster bleats sinister, heart-synched polyrhythms.

The Maid has inflamed eyes and nattering teeth. Her clothes split at the seams and shed to the floor. Her obese and voluptuous body is a patchwork of crazy-quilt skin. Her eyes and teeth in close-up descend on Bubbles in pixilated slo-mo.

The Maid holds Bubbles tightly around the waist. She absorbs Bubbles' flesh into her own. The two grind pube to pube.

SFX: Echo the fall and rise of Bubbles' high-pitched, staccato sighs.

Zoom to close-up of Bubbles' eyes during her final spasmodic screech. Spin-wipe to:

EXT. Cotton field of the Old South—Day.

Toothless OLD COONS strum Happy Nigger Banjo Tunes for dancing PICKANINNIES slapping hambone on their knees and thighs.

Reverse spin-wipe to:

INT. Brownstone—Attic—Night.

Zoom out from close-up of eyes to medium shot of Bubbles.

BUBBLES
(screaming)

Ride it, Lightnin'!

A hard wave of convulsions thunders through the Maid as she falls to the floor. Her teeth gnash. Her limbs thrash. The boom blaster's computerized Petro-rhythms pound concurrently with her disjointed movements.

Her head, arms, hands, legs, and feet move with an independence of their own. They begin to talk, change shape, and emit sounds: Music. Radio white noise. Reptile skin. A bird's head. A cat with a coat of flames. TV commercials. Radio white noise. The BERNHARD GOETZ confession mixed to hip-hop rap rhythms. Pentecostal tent-house shouts. Police sirens. MALCOLM X speeches. Harlem bar talk. The bark of heroin pitchmen. The assassination of JOHN F. KENNEDY cross-edited with the *Amos and Andy* radio show. And the recurrent image of a YOUNG BLACK BOY repeating the phrase, *"Yo, man! You got five dollars? Yo, man! You got five dollars?"* answered with gunfire.

The Maid's convulsions subside. She pants with exhaustion. A RAT scurries from the shadows, sits on her heaving bosom, and cleans its whiskers. The maid's eyelids snap open with the rat trained in the cross-hairs of her vision. She spits like a cat.

The rat leaps from her bosom and wriggles down a hole in the attic's floor. The Maid scrambles into a four-legged position on her hands and knees. She arches her back and mewls. Lifting the attic's door, the Maid disappears down the stairs.

Bubbles dangles alone in the darkness.

The sounds of breaking furniture, crashing glass, and a hissing cat filter through the floorboards. The rat's terrified squeal is heard offscreen.

MAID
(o.s.)

Ahah! Gotcha!

SFX: Death squeal, ripping flesh, and crunching bone.

MAID
(o.s.)

Uuuum—mm-mmm! Lawd hab mercy! Raw rat-haid innards!

SFX: *Suck! Suck! Slurp! Slurp! Smack! Smack!*

MAID
(o.s.)

Nah where d'res ob dat reefas? Here it is! 'N' its d'stick! No stems! No seeds! Not nary a leaf! Jus' a long pretty braid o' choice Jamaican buds! Roll dese bad boys up, turn on wif Cab 'n' ah be ready fo' Freddy! Hah!

A sheaf of cigarette paper crinkles. A match ignites into flame. A sharp, sibilant intake of breath. The slap of a record on a turntable. And the voice of Marlene Dietrich singing "Hot Voodoo" blares through the speakers.

MAID
(o.s.)

*Dat ain't Cab! Dis' dat blond Venus Nazi ho bitch
singin' dat phony hoodoo song she sang in a gorilla suit
'mongst all dem big-lipped jungle Niggas! Ain't dis
'bout o' blip! Dat chile try'n drape me wif m'own shit!
Well wait to dat bellydonna gits into her ass! Ha! Huh?*

The Marlene Dietrich recording skips, repeating:

MARLENE DIETRICH
(o.s.)

Hot Voodoo…! Hot Voodoo…!
Hot Voodoo…! Hot Voodoo…!

MAID
(o.s.)

*Wha' da fuck?! M'hands! Deys meltin'! 'N' m'feet! Deys
meltin', too!*

There is an unearthly wail of anguish.

MAID
(o.s.)

*Oh, Lawd! M'face done turned to snot 'n' commenced
t'drippin' off d'bone! Oh, Lawd! Hep me, Jesus! Hep
me! Hep me! Ah's wastin' away! Hep me, Jesus! Hep
me! Hep me!*

Tilt up Bubbles' glistening body through mists of incense
and candle flames.

BUBBLES
(v.o.)

And there I dangled, in the attic, quietly
hallucinating amid vile odors and strange Negro

figurines. On the floor below, the maid had gone mad—her blubbersome black bulk flopping and flailing about the floor, bellowing for a pink-skinned god who would never come. In her superstitious Negro narcosis, she believed her end was near, and all that would be left of her would be a puddle of bubbling black bile with two eyeballs floating at the ends of their tendrils. If only she had taken the precaution of wearing a pair of rubber gloves. Or had simply wiped the unguent from her hands. She hadn't. Instead, she chose to underestimate the power of the Blond Venus.

Dolly in for close shot of Bubbles's face.

The ceiling's termite-burrowed beams splinter and collapse under the strain of Bubbles' chains. In a rain of rotted wood, plaster, and steel links, she falls to the floor, landing crouched on the balls of her toes. Dazed but alert, Bubbles searches through the debris.

BUBBLES
(v.o.)

The belladonna bucked and kicked in like a mule. But I hadn't been a Deadhead for nothing.

I knew those thorny, vine-entangled wilds of psychedelia as well as I knew the mystical significance of the lines on my own hand. After all, even if he was a fat, over-forty beer fart, I did suck off Jerry Garcia.

Bubbles finds the key to the handcuffs in the Maid's pile of shredded clothing. She unlocks the cuffs and stands, shaking the circulation back into her hands. She rummages through the attic's trunks and boxes, finding a two-piece leopardskin bikini and an old electric razor.

First stroking the bikini's cheap fuzzy fabric, Bubbles ties herself into the bikini bottom and knots the bikini's top. Walking to the ritual area, she takes a hand mirror scrawled with modern petrodesigns, and places it on top of a trunk. She plugs in the electric razor and shaves her scalp peach-fuzz short, leaving the shock of hair arcing over her brow.

BUBBLES
(v.o.)

Even with the jumble of coke smoke and other shit, the belladonna head didn't seem much different from a jimsonweed high.

Bubbles lifts her eyes to the ceiling, as she pulls her arms through the sleeves of her black leather jacket, and stares into the light of a bright full moon, balancing her Wayfarer shades on the bridge of her nose.

BUBBLES
(v.o.)

I found some jimsonweed at school once, a whole field of it, behind my dorm. And what happened next was like what happened to that village in France that flipped from ergot poisoning. Or like that scene in *Wild in the Streets* with Shelley Winters shaking her fat ass on a headful of acid in a concentration camp for the over thirty.

Turning over the objects in the Maid's temple, Bubbles drags a trunk across the floor and places it under the hole in the ceiling. She mounts the trunk and pulls herself through the hole.

BUBBLES
(v.o.)

What it wasn't like was Woodstock. I'd hoped that bird on the fucking poster keeled over from strychnine poisoning.

Bubbles stands on the brownstone's roof and scans the skyline. Bands of ALLEY CATS roam the rooftops.

> **BUBBLES**
> *(v.o.)*
> Once, I threw a Jonestown Kool-Aid party, and painted a big messy mural of that stupid fucking bird, with two X's for eyes, hanging upside down on the neck of a guitar. Then I strung black lights and spiked the punch with acid.
>
> It's the closest thing you can get to cyanide and still have a good time.

With the moon looming large and luminous above the skyline and Cats flocking underfoot, Bubbles leaps from roof to roof with swiftness, agility, and athletic grace.

> **BUBBLES**
> *(v.o.)*
> If you've ever copped in Washington Square Park, you know what I mean...

The Cats descend fire escapes, wind through alleys—

> **BUBBLES**
> *(v.o.)*
> Still, tripping to a cassette of the Jonestown death screams with a roomful of black-light-blind Oi Boys somersaulting overhead isn't half as frightening as what happened to us after eating that field of jimsonweed.

—and jump, finally, through the paneless windows of an abandoned factory.

BUBBLES
(v.o.)

One girl stained her entire body green by rolling around in the grass. She moved out of her dorm, and lived on the shore of a nearby stream without a stitch of clothes. She brought all of her furniture, too—including a four-poster bed and a full dining room set. Another student's girlfriend died. He had fucked the corpse several times over the course of three days before he realized what had happened.

The skyline's industrial configuration of stone, steel, and smoke loses its aspect of modernity in the ancientness of night. DESOLATE FIGURES are reduced to grotesque primeval forms with strange geometries of moonlight and shadow. Cruel machineries grind pinwheels of flame. Sludge churns in the harbor. Tugboats bleat in the fog.

BUBBLES
(v.o.)

Trying to navigate with belladonna in your blood is like trying to sustain a thought on really shitty smack. Forget detachment and well-being. Think nausea and stupidity. And not just your basic weed-bed, feeble-head, dunce-cap stupidity either. But monumental stupidity in all its awesome klieg-light wonder. Try and imagine the complete collapse of the higher functions—the simple failure of brain—coupled with a tightening net of pain wrapped around your bowels. Imagine a host of stillborn phantoms reeling before the mind's eye. Imagine all this. And the long Negro night ahead.

But, like I said, I hadn't been a Deadhead for nothing.

Bubbles, too, descends fire escapes, winds through alleys, and climbs on the window ledge of the abandoned factory.

INT. Paint Factory—Night.

With her figure silhouetted by the moon in the mouth of the window frame, its light casting her in a halo fringed by glass fangs, Bubbles kicks the remaining shards of glass from the window's lower half, scattering slivers through the gloom.

Climbing over the ledge, Bubbles drops to the floor, raising a swirl of phosphorescent fairy dust around her. She coughs phlegm and grit into the cup of her fist.

Peering over the plane of her Wayfarer frames, Bubbles stares into the surrounding darkness.

The floor of the factory is heaped with radiant piles of paint pigment. Misty and eerily luminous, the piles spill in all directions, joined by a confluence of vaporous, variegated lines.

Phosphorescent paw prints track the dust over the floor. Green eyes gleam in the gloom. And multiply in kaleidoscopic unfoldment.

Glyphs shift in and out of focus, in a fuzzy, fluorescent glow, squirming with repellent underlife, as if maggots feeding in the furrows of moldering flesh.

Bubbles withdraws her straight razor from her jacket's inside pocket, casually noting the color of her hand. Her once white flesh is now a dusky violet. Staring down at her legs, she finds the same dusky hue. Knitting her brow in curiosity, she looks up at the vaulted ceiling.

Entangled in a confusion of soot-encrusted cables, a network of black lights are strung high above the floor.

Agitated tails thrash. Bubbles pivots on the balls of her toes. Her straight razor whisks open and glimmers in the black-light glow.

HUNDREDS OF CATS—all black with gleaming green eyes—pace to and fro. PUSSIES IN HEAT point asses in the air, drag bellies across the ground, and push forepaws along the floor. TOM CATS pounce and pump.

Mysterious paw prints materialize and phosphoresce.

Under scrawled squiggles on the factory's far wall, Bubbles deciphers the words:

BUSH MASTER PAINT FACTORY

The letters permute in shape. The scrawl slithers to the outer edges of the wall, circling in a nimbus of shimmering spermatozoa. The geometric permutations shift with mechanical precision, pinwheeling into a disk of vibrancy and color.

A square turns counterclockwise within the circumference of the disk. Inside the square, a triangle revolves on its axis.

The mandala spins faster and faster. And a whirl of demonic images are twice reflected on the surfaces of Bubbles' shades.

The scrawl slithers down the wall and undulates across the floor, swimming up Bubbles' thighs.

Shuddering in disgust, Bubbles flings herself to the floor and lands in a pile of effulgent dust.

Dropping her straight razor, Bubbles pinches herself in hysteria. Her Wayfarers fly from her face.

The scrawl fades under her touch. The cats yowl in chorus. Ice-blue static bristles across the floor.

Bubbles is tossed up from the ground. Spun around. Dashed down. Repeatedly. Painfully. In stroboscopic thrash-dance. A chromatic blur of blood and pigment. Flung, finally, into the pit of smoking pigment, a ghost in iridescent colors.

Bubbles spins around the pit's rim as she's sucked into the eye of its vortex.

One by one, the Cats leap through the air and vanish into the luminous, vapor-spewing mounds.

INT. Pit.

Down the Rabbit's Rectum

Bubbles somersaults through the pit's smoking underside, diving through the darkness. With outswept arms, she rides the currents of air with the buoyancy of a paper kite.

A sinuous slash of black powder cuts diagonally across her face, highlighting the gemlike luster of her eyes. The feathered puff of hair blowing over her brow is dusted a soft blue and stippled with a firefly glow of yellow and green

Bubbles talks aloud to herself, her voice tinged with an undertone of panic.

> **BUBBLES**
> This isn't real, right? I'm having a hallucination, and this really isn't happening. I'm actually sitting in the booth of a dingy Lower Eastside bar, nodding out on some Puerto Rican dope.

Spectral bodies tumble through the abyss. Feline sounds resound. Jagged, ice-blue webs of electricity flash in the background.

> **BUBBLES**
> I feel safe. I feel protected. My cool is beyond question. There are white people here. Flesh and blood white people. Elvis's own white people, strengthed by the courage of booze and jukebox rock and roll.

What wool-headed hipster in his right mind wants an encounter of the drunken, Caucasoid kind?

I can keep my head together. I'm in control. It's just a drug in my body.

Relax. Breathe deeply.

Her mouth gapes in realization.

BUBBLES
Omigod! *I forgot how to breathe!*

INT. Pit.

The Cave of the Flaming Tar Babies

Contorting like a drowning swimmer, Bubbles slams the pit's clay floor with a bounce—*ooff!*—landing on her rump in a ring of tar-colored DWARVES with sagging toadlike skin; bulbous heads; bulging lemon-shaped eyes; and plump, red lips framing a bow of gleaming, yellow teeth. Uncircumsized penises poke out from beneath pitted potbellies. Bubbles offers a reluctant smile.

BUBBLES

Let me guess. *The Antipathies,* right?

Twittering their tongues against their teeth, the Dwarves stand Bubbles on her feet.

BUBBLES

Hmmmm. The short twittering types.

Bubbles' brow furrows in sudden curiosity. She sniffs the air.

BUBBLES

What's that smell?

She places her hands on the shoulders of the Dwarf standing below her, bends over, and licks the top of his head.

BUBBLES

Yuck! Nasty ol' coon candy! It looks like doo-doo! It tastes like doo-doo! I hate licorice!

Wiping her mouth on the sleeve of her black leather jacket, Bubbles pulls the zipper of her breast pocket open and takes out a fistful of humanoid fudge figurines. With a grimace of disgust, she tosses the candies into her mouth like a handful of Spanish peanuts. Her teeth turn brown with saliva and chocolate.

The LICORICE MEN stare in wonder. Bubbles spits into her hand and extends her palm, offering the few half-chewed chocolates in her hand.

BUBBLES

Want some?

Sensing a distinct familial link between themselves and the cluster of mangled fudge faces in the cup of Bubbles' palm, the Licorice Men fling their arms in the air with a squeal of revulsion and trundle away in the echoing darkness.

Bubbles is left standing alone in the stalactite-roofed cavern.

BUBBLES

I guess they weren't ready for the fruits of the White Man's technology. *Or Muhammad's message to the New Black Man...!*

FADE

INT. Cave—Night.

Emerging from an opening between the cavern's walls, her eyes seemingly suspended in darkness, sparkling with the inflamed radiance of precious stones, Bubbles' mouth falls open in shock.

Manacled to the walls on each side of the cavern's widening passageway, in varying states of thaw and decay, are a dozen pudgy DOUGHBOYS—the pale spherical fellows pictured on the cylindrical packages located in the supermarket's frozen-food department.

The Licorice Men release ONE OF THE DOUGHBOYS from his manacles. They lift him off the wall and carry him through the cavern. The Doughboy kicks and screams. He cries in a high thin voice—

DOUGHBOY

*No! No! Anything but that! The briar patch!! But,
please, no—*NOT THE FLAMING TAR BABY!

LICORICE MEN

Chortle. Chortle. Chortle.

Bubbles panics and runs but finds no route of escape. Concealing herself in shadow, she flattens herself against the wall. Edging along its hard, uneven surface, she smears A HALF-DOZEN DOUGHBOYS in her wake—mouths groaning black ovals, eyes anguished crow's feet, gray paste spurting from deflated bellies in conical turdlike piles—leaving a stucco surface of squashed limbs and flat, disfigured faces.

67

She nears the ring of Licorice Men, hiding behind a large rock.

Inside the licorice ring, the Doughboy cowers. The Licorice Men punch and kick him about the cavern like a beach ball. The Doughboy snuffles back a bubble of mucus, crying *boo-hoo-hoo*. The Licorice Men mimic his suffering and laugh at his neutered crotch.

The Doughboy is kicked to the ground. He pleads for his life.

DOUGHBOY

There were *deals* made! *Lies* told! It was the *corporation's* decision! I was just a pawn! A trademark! *A mere promotional symbol!* But I fell into the wrong hands! A team of unscrupulous animators! It could have been anyone! The Marshmallow Puff-Head! The Riddlin' Rubber Man! Mr. Creme Bean! Even the Selzer Kidd! *Anyone!*

The Licorice Men turn to each other and snicker. The circle parts. The Doughboy screams—

DOUGHBOY

No! Please! Don't! My wife has a bun in the oven! She's French! *A croissant!* You can have her! I'll even throw in a wheel of Brie and a bottle of Bordeaux Grand Cru!

Scrambling about the ground on hands and knees, the Doughboy runs in circles like a wounded pup. His body swells in size and ripples with a spasm of violent hiccups.

DOUGHBOY

Hic! Excuse me! Hic! Hic!

68

The Licorice Men cackle. The Doughboy looks up. His face twists in terror.

A cork-eyed TAR BABY, wearing roped burlap pants and a plaid flannel shirt, totters through the shadows on awkward wooden legs. A corncob pipe is thrust in its button mouth. A straw skimmer is cocked rakishly on its sticky, domed head.

The Doughboy cringes with fright. His face wrinkles in woe.

DOUGHBOY

NO! NO! NOT THE TAR BABY—!

Entering through an opening in the circle, the Tar Baby stumbles toward the Doughboy like a toddler taking its first uncertain steps. It falls on the Doughboy and ignites in a whirl of flames. The fire burns with crackling vigor and dies away. The Tar Baby crumbles into a bed of fine, gray ash. A pile of eight dozen unbuttered biscuits lie buried beneath the mound.

Pinwheeling through the air like a team of championship midget wrestlers, the Licorice Men quickly pounce on the pile. They stuff their jowls with biscuits, spitting sprays of crumbs.

Screwing his face into a knot of concentration, ONE OF THE LICORICE MEN inserts a biscuit into the split of his ass and farts. The biscuit shoots across the cavern trailing in a plume of dark rectal exhaust.

The Licorice Man grins. He looks like Louie Armstrong.

LICORICE MAN

Poppin' fresh!

Packing bulbs of baked bread dough between the cheeks of their twisting black behinds, the Licorice Men twitter and wiggle and bleat cacophonies of moist brown sounds. Dozens of biscuits sail through the air, coated with tremulant slime.

Shaded in obscurity, Bubbles strikes a match and tosses it into the cavern. The Licorice Men shriek as their asses flare in jets of blue flame. Bubbles escapes unnoticed in the confusion.

And Tar Baby, he ain't sayin' nothin'...

INT. Cave

Paws patter along the cavern's floor like a soft spring rain and stop before a set of large casket doors. Gaseous ether rises from the ground, and ghostly feline forms leap through the solid oak.

Bubbles propels herself from the wall, running the length of the cavern. She stops at the set of doors, placing her hand on the knob. Slowly opening a door, she steps inside. The door closes with a hollow, reverberating crunch.

FADE

After years of bouncing Miss Sally's grandson on his lap, Uncle Remus could no longer resist the temptation.

With his eyeballs distended and agoggle, his trousers piled at his ankles, and his sagging buttocks exposed, Uncle Remus shuffled his withered organ between the cheeks of the child's smooth white bottom. He popped his fingers to spectral moke music.

"Honey chil', han' yo' po' Unca Remus dat dere jar ob Brer Bear Grease. *Yeah!* Dat's it! *Slap it an' slick it!* Now ROLL DAT BONE!"

Miss Sally walked in on Uncle Remus and her grandchild unannounced, and fainted dead away.

Needless to say, Uncle Remus' arthritic legs hobbled in the direction of the North Star.

—*The Untold Tales of Uncle Remus*

INT.—Church of Uncle H. Rap Remus.

Dusted in the paint pigment's multicolored overlays, Bubbles stands inside the cavernous interior of the church with the casket doors looming behind her. She peers over the plane of her dark-lensed Wayfarers.

Under the high, concave ceiling, which is painted with pictures of dreaded, spliff-smoking, chocolate-skinned cherubim, restless throngs of RASTAFARIANS clothed in black leopard-head-hooded animal-hair hides, with withered white penile organs woven into the ends of their tangled dreads, face the stage at the rear of the church and wave clawed leopard paws mounted on wooden clubs in a fit of tribal frenzy.

An enormous poster of a bug-eyed black man in a stovepipe hat and a star-spangled, red, white, and blue striped suit hangs above the stage. He is crouched in a stoop with his trousers heaped around his ankles and his hands propped on his knees, holding a bar of butter in his right fist. He looks over his shoulder with a broad and toothless grin, offering his wrinkled buttocks in a coquettish pose. The poster exclaims in big block letters:

UNCLE SAMBO WANTS YOU!

Below the poster, UNCLE H. RAP REMUS, an arthritic old Negro dressed in green paramilitary fatigues, with gnarled gray dreads flopping on each side of his otherwise bald head, holds a luger P.08 to Uncle Sambo's woolly skull.

UNCLE H. RAP REMUS

What was his crime against the REVOLUTION?!

LEOPARD MEN

He wanted his hot cakes greased!

UNCLE H. RAP REMUS

We all know what Uncle Sambo wants to do to
you, but what do *you* want to do to *Uncle Sambo*?

LEOPARD MEN

Grease 'im!

Uncle H. Rap Remus pulls the Luger's trigger and Uncle
Sambo's head explodes in a geyser of blood, bone, and burr.
His corpse flops to the floor and is kicked from the stage.

UNCLE H. RAP REMUS

GREASED!

Thunderous applause rolls through the church. The Uncle
Sambo poster is eaten away in the sudden appearance of
flames. Underneath is a rear-screen projection of Idi Amin
Dada. It reads:

IDI SEZ: "FIST 'EM HARD AND FIST 'EM DEEP!

The applause subsides. The stage lights dim. The church is
cast in shadow. A single spot is lit for Uncle H. Rap Remus.
He stalks the stage with mike in hand.

74

UNCLE H. RAP REMUS

Bruthas 'n' sistas, the Whyte Man is a Crazy Man.
Must I repeat myself? I said, "The Whyte Man is
a Crazy Man."

Yeah. He crazy. Got to be.

The Whyte Man, the Crazy Man, has the nuclear
capacity to kill hissef hundreds of times over,
blowin' ever'body 'n' ever'thang SKY HIGH!

And there is no rational answer why. *Except—*

The Whyte Man, the Crazy Man, wants to die.

'Cause he crazy, see? Got to be.

The Whyte Man, the Crazy Man, has what
psychoanalysts call a *"death wish"*—a wish to *die*.

The Whyte Man, the Crazy Man, is the single
greatest defiler of the planet on the planet. He
has polluted the air, the water, and the minds of
his children. He has even poisoned the very land
in which he grows his food.

Now only a man with a "wish to die" would jump
on his dining table, unload the contents of his
bowels, and proceed to eat it.

This explains why the Whyte Man's mind is
poison. Have you ever looked inside a Whyte
Man's brain, bruthas 'n' sistas?

The X ray of a skull appears on the rear-projection screen.
The skull is filled with a ring of turds. A cloud of flies buzz
inside.

UNCLE H. RAP REMUS

You know how the Whyte Man complains of
ringing in the ears?

That's not ringing, bruthas 'n' sistas. That's the
sound of *flies* feeding off the lump of *offal* the
Whyte Man calls a brain.

Pardon my language, bruthas 'n' sistas, but with
shit for brains, how could anyone believe the
Whyte Man is *superior*? Even *he know* he inferior.
Why else would he want to blow hissef up?

Obviously, bruthas 'n' sistas, we don't need
anybody like that with us on this planet.

The screen fades to black. Swirling to a slow, reggae back-
beat, WRAITHLIKE FIGURES drone in sepulchral voices.

HAUNTED VOICES
All Whyte People
Pitch over
And die
Now!

All Whyte People
Pitch over
And die
Now!

All Whyte People
Pitch over
And die
Now!

UNCLE H. RAP REMUS
Puke blood!   Swell up!   Turn purple!

HAUNTED VOICES
All Whyte People
Pitch over
And die
Now!

76

All Whyte People
Pitch over
And die
Now!

All Whyte People
Pitch over
And die
Now!

UNCLE H. RAP REMUS

As Aminites, we believe the living incarnation of God on Earth is not Haile Selassie, *but* IDI AMIN DADA, *who, in his wisdom, created Whyte People so Black People could take advantage of them!*

HAUNTED VOICES

All Whyte People
Pitch over
And die
Now!

UNCLE H. RAP REMUS

As Aminites, we wear the Whyte Man's withered organs in our hair, to absorb his power, to end his spawn!

HAUNTED VOICES

All Whyte People
Pitch over
And die
Now!

UNCLE H. RAP REMUS

As Aminites, we believe in the INALIENABLE *right of all Whyte People to self-combust! Ignite like match heads! Burst into a howling ball of flame!*

HAUNTED VOICES

All Whyte People
Pitch over
And die
Now!

UNCLE H. RAP REMUS

Or Our Flaming Tar Baby bombs will stick to your skin like napalm!

HAUNTED VOICES

All Whyte People
Pitch over
And die
Now!

UNCLE H. RAP REMUS

As Aminites, we have one pledge and one pledge only!
WHAT'S THAT PLEDGE?!

The mob of Leopard Men salute with mounted claws.

LEOPARD MEN

Fist 'em hard! Fist 'em deep!

UNCLE H. RAP REMUS

WHAT'S THAT PLEDGE?!

LEOPARD MEN

Fist 'em hard! Fist 'em deep!

UNCLE H. RAP REMUS

LOUDER!

LEOPARD MEN

Fist 'em hard! Fist 'em deep!

UNCLE H. RAP REMUS

I can't hear you!

LEOPARD MEN

Fist 'em hard! Fist 'em deep!

UNCLE H. RAP REMUS

That's right! Fist 'em hard! Fist 'em deep!

The house lights brighten. The wraithlike singers disappear. Uncle H. Rap Remus's eye is caught by Bubbles' bobbing boobs. His tongue snaps over his lips in undisguised lechery.

UNCLE H. RAP REMUS

I see we have been joined tonight by one who seeks initiation into our fold.

Bubbles twitches and gesticulates like a Kangoled Krac Kidd in solid-gold chains.

BUBBLES

Yeah. *Naw.* I'm jus' *chillin*—y'know—*slummin', bummin', 'n' checkin' it out!* An' hey, yo', I'm down wit'chall—from back here! *Word up!*

Bubbles displays her teeth in a sheepish grin, thrusting her fist in the air. Her bosom wobbles with a saucy quiver.

No, sister, come join us. Your skin is emblematic
of all colors. Unblended, perhaps, but Dada's
color. God's color. Join us. Become one of us.

Shaking their mounted paws to the rising rhythms of the
conga drums, the Leopard Men chant:

LEOPARD MEN

Ooga-booga! Booga-ooga! We accept her. We
accept her. One of us. One of us. We will make
you one of us. Ooga-booga. Booga-ooga. One of
us. One of us. We will make you one of us.

The Leopard Men surround Bubbles, lift her off the floor,
and carry her hand over head toward the stage. Springing
like a jack-in-the-box in the confusion of arms and hands, a
cocoa-colored PINHEAD in a polka-dot nightshirt, wearing a
single, ribboned dread on top of his head, fires a plastic
popgun. Its brightly colored ball bounces off of Bubbles'
nose.

PINHEAD

Ooga-booga backward!

Two Licorice Men stand on the edge of the crowd. Each
wears a black leopardskin tunic held together by a single
over-the-shoulder strap. One wears a bowler and sucks on
the stub of an unlit cigar.

LICORICE LEOPARD MAN IN BOWLER

Fist 'em hard. Fist 'em deep, brutha!

SECOND LICORICE LEOPARD MAN

Right on! I'm tired o' sittin' on d'bottom shelf o'
d'candy case, passed over for a muthafuckin' box

o' bref mints! I ain't nobody's nigga baby no mo'!
From now on, my politically correct self-
definition is *Congolese Confection*—the
revolutionary sweet designed to kill whytey! Eat
me, baby, an' you one dead hunkie! *Shee-it! A
muthafuck a muthafuckin' bref mint!*

LICORICE LEOPARD MAN IN BOWLER
Right on right on!

Bubbles is passed from groping hand to groping hand. Black
fingers defile her every orifice. The dreaded Leopard Men
sniff their fingers with lascivious laughs. Bubbles' brow is
bunched into a wry frown. Her left cheek is lumped into a
half smile.

BUBBLES
If you insist on poking your fingers where they're
clearly not wanted, *you could at least rub a little
faster!*

The center-stage section of the floor slides open with an
electric hum, revealing a rectangular pool of water. Sitting in
a cradle of hands formed by the Leopard Men, Bubbles is
swung from the floor and into the pool. A column of water
splashes the stage. Her Wayfarers bounce from her head and
sink to the bottom of the pool. Uncle H. Rap Remus shuffles
his feet, swings his arms, and claps his hands with the
unbridled enthusiasm of a chittlin'-circuit Holy Roller.

UNCLE H. RAP REMUS
We gwine wash dis wayward chile! We gwine slap
d'whyte man's stains from her soul! An' den she
be ready to come for Dada!

81

Bubbles sits upright in the pool, blinking water from her eyes. The paint pigments dusting her skin begin to run. Colors converge.

> **UNCLE H. RAP REMUS**
> *Dada be praised!*

Uncle H. Rap Remus smacks Bubbles on the forehead with the palm of his hand. *Hard.* The blow knocks Bubbles below the surface of the water. Bubbles springs back like an inflated boppo-doll, sputtering water and gasping for air. She coughs. And a WORM—fat, black, and flat-headed—arcs from her mouth. It sails through the air, landing in the pool with a splash. It wiggles across the water. Uncle H. Rap Remus smacks her again. *Thwack!*

> **UNCLE H. RAP REMUS**
> *Dada be praised!*

Bubbles bobs back and forth in a daze. Her belly heaves with spasms. She gags. And another WORM twirls from her mouth. *Splish!*

Uncle H. Rap Remus slaps her for the third and final time.

> **UNCLE H. RAP REMUS**
> DADA BE PRAISED!

Bubbles disappears into the pool. Air bubbles gurgle to the top. The water is muddy with pigment. Uncle H. Rap Remus stares into the murky pool. The air bubbles slowly disappear. He turns to his followers. His expression is wrought with sorrow.

> **UNCLE H. RAP REMUS**
> Bruthas 'n' sistas, Dada has a higher purpose in
> mind. He has claimed this nubile young neophyte

with the hefty bosom for his own. It is not for us
to question his mysteries or ways. Let us pray.

All heads bow in silence. The two Congolese Confections sob
in each other's arms with thick rivulets of mucus dripping
from their nostrils.

The bowlered Confection's eyeballs distend in disbelief. The
cigar stub drops from his mouth.

CONFECTION IN BOWLER

*Great gugga-mugga 'n' jumpin' Jehoshophats! Does we
get to fist dat too?!*

Bubbles sits upright in the pool. The water has washed away
the coats of powdered pigment, unmasking the true color of
her skin.

Needless to say, the natives are restless.

The Leopard Men pound threatening rhythms on their
conga drums, grunt indecipherable gibberish, and sharpen
the claws of their mounted leopard paws. Some drag their
knuckles on the ground in a drunken, apish ring dance,
trailed by animal pelts hanging from the tails of their spines.
The Leopard Men's chant drones through the church with an
insistent hum.

LEOPARD MEN

Fist 'em hard! Fist 'em deep!
Fist 'em hard! Fist 'em deep!
Fist 'em hard! Fist 'em deep!

A small, nude, uncircumsized BLACK BOY circulates through
the crowd with a bucket of lard. The Leopard Men shove
their fists into the bucket and massage the stiff, pale blobs
into their skin.

Crawling from the pool, Bubbles stumbles about the stage on hands and knees. Her stomach heaves with violent contractions. Uncle H. Rap Remus backs away in revulsion. The dreaded Leopard Men surge toward the stage. Faces blur into animal fur.

Bubbles' back buckles and folds up like a cheap lawn chair. Heaving again, she unfolds into a four-on-the-floor doggie pose. Her belly bloats to pregnant proportions and her skin shimmers with a golden underlight. A silver nimbus circles her head.

Her mouth a green rictus of salivating sickness, Bubbles turns toward the clamoring, claw-wielding Leopard Men in surreal slo-mo. A yellow spray obstructs her view.

On the edge of the stage, the small black boy stands in Bubbles' line of vision. His belly protrudes. His legs bend slightly at the knees. Urine dribbles from his stubby, uncircumsized cock.

Bubbles' tongue reaches out from her mouth. And she vomits. Worms. In great cresting waves.

Splattered with squirming slime and slither, the small black boy is knocked from the stage. He hits the floor—*hard*—buried under a mass of writhing putrescence.

Backing away from the stage, the Leopard Men grunt and gesture in superstitious awe at the retching, golden-hued BEETLE-GIRL.

His dreads untangled, shooting in electric shocks from the sides of his head, a chatter-toothed Uncle H. Rap Remus sits cringing on the floor in the wings of the stage. He clutches the microphone close to his chest.

Watching his flock retreat in fear, Uncle H. Rap Remus quickly regains his composure. He stands, points a finger at Bubbles, and speaks in a commanding voice into his microphone.

UNCLE H. RAP REMUS

Ignore this bile-spuming demon spawn!

The Leopard Men stare at their leader in quizzical bemusement.

UNCLE H. RAP REMUS

Our only hope to save ourselves, bruthas 'n' sistas—*is to pass the plate!*

Bubbles turns to Uncle H. Rap Remus, her face an ever darkening green...

UNCLE H. RAP REMUS

Dig deep into your pockets! Let me see your palms shine with *gold!*

...And *gobs* him in a torrent of undulating worm vomit!

Uncle H. Rap Remus's eyes stare large, round, and white from within the slithering black heap.

UNCLE H. RAP REMUS

Dis am regustin'...!

TWO WORMS with gnashing, nightmare teeth chew holes through his pupils and leap from his eye sockets. The HEAP OF WORMS caves in on itself and leaves a writhing chalk-white skeleton.

SFX: The wet, thrusting sound of a vigorous cock slish-sloshing a bubbling cunt filtered through an electronic wind tunnel.

With her legs bent at the knees and her feet thrown in the air. Bubbles lies on her back, rolling and grinding her ass against the floor.

Her skin's radiant underlight turns a dark olive green and her swollen beetle belly deflates. Wrinkled nodules the size and shape of small walnuts sprout on her legs and chest, ripping through her leopard-spotted bra. They swell to three times their original size and erupt, spurting a milky, green pus.

Big-lipped, cotton-topped, and broad-nostriled HEADS pop from the pustular pods, blinking mucus from their large, rolling eyes.

TWO BURRHEADS, grinning in fish-eyed close-up, supplant Bubbles' Brazil-nut nipples. Showing off rows of straight white teeth, the Burrheads lock eyes with Bubbles.

RIGHT BURRHEAD

Say, Lefty, how do you babysit a Niggerhead?

LEFT BURRHEAD

I don't know, Mister Tit-Top. How do you babysit
a Niggerhead?

RIGHT BURRHEAD

You lick its lips and stick it to the wall!

The boob-top Burrheads cross their eyes and stick out their tongues, expelling razzberries of spit and air.

The other Burrheads in bloom on Bubbles' bod peal with slaughterhouse squeals and spring from their burrows of ulcerated flesh, leaving a trail of mucus and pus. Thick, muscular tails extend from their necks. They slap the floor of the stage. *Thwack!*

Bubbles' wounds mysteriously heal. And her color returns to normal.

The WORMS wiggling in the scattered puke piles grow larger and larger. Their heads inflate and form faces. They rear up on the tips of their tails, open their mouths and *screech!*

The Leopard Men panic. Pandemonium prevails.

They flee in confusion. Withered penises fly in all directions. Club claws are flung to the floor. CHILDREN are trampled underfoot. Blood spurts. Eyeballs fly. Intestines dangle.

Bubbles fishes her Wayfarers from the pool, rolls to her feet, and leaps from the stage. She drops to the floor, adjusts her shades, and runs through the crowd. The horde of squealing NEGROID VOMITOIDS slither in pursuit.

Bubbles cuts a path through the surrounding chaos. The Leopard Men bow in supplication. And the supplicants, in ecstatic reverential awe, are devoured by the squealing hordes.

INT. Underground passageways.

Backlit in silhouette, Bubbles wings through a maze of cragged passageways with the echo of human pain howling behind her.

Soon, a circle of light looms at the end of a tunnel. Bubbles runs in its direction, exulting in its brilliance, her ankled feet rattling in rhythm with her pounding heart.

A harsh whisking sound skitters across the ground. And a horde of Negroid Vomitoids turn into the passage, squealing and grunting and nattering their teeth.

Bubbles leaps through the light, landing on her feet in the lurid glare of Times Square.

The squealing Negroid Vomitoids slither through the opening of a sewer drainpipe, slapping to the ground with a sick wet sound.

Bubbles quickly runs through the doors of the 42nd Street Multiplex Grindhouse.

The 42nd Street Multiplex Grindhouse's marquee reads:

"THE ROCKY-HORROR NEGRO SHOW"

INT. Multiplex Grindhouse—Night.

Bubbles sits in the theater's semidarkened auditorium with an outlaw bandana tied around the lower half of her face, surrounded by a sea of bulbous SOFT-SCULPTURE FACES with a topiary of fluorescent, grafittilike wildstyle designs cut into the fountains of hair flowing from their cotton-stuffed skulls.

As music swells, the muppetlike audience sways in happy-face sing-along. MALCOM X'S CADAVER strolls onstage. Maggots squirm in his jellied eyeholes.

MALCOM X

Hi! My name is El-Hajj Malik El-Shabazz.
Remember me? I was shot back in the sixties.

He sprinkles a handful of sand onstage, shuffles his feet in soft-shoe, and sings.

MALCOLM X

It's astounding
Time is fleeting
Ideas are getting old.
So listen closely—
We haven't got very much longer.
Fictions have taken hold.
You think—
"Consciousness rising!"
But I say—
"Worms are writhing!"
Eating your very soul!

Now I remember,
Eatin' that *swine pork*,
When *blackness* hit me
And a Voice called—
"Never mo'!"

No mo' pig tails
From another
Dimension.
Or eatin' ham hocks
With mystical
Pretensions.

Pork is
A Whyte Devil God's
Invention
To hinder
The Black Man's
Ascension!

AUDIENCE

Don't eat the swine pork again!

MALCOLM X

You feel a sensation. It's
Black frustration. And you
Cop another bag of sedation.
Then you realize it's just
Another form of castration.

But after losing the coke dip,
Or slipping the duji chip, and getting
Out of the swine trip, you will
Never be the same.

I speak to you
From another dimension

Addressing
Your Afrocentric intentions.
Well-secluded
I see all.

AUDIENCE

Don't eat the swine pork again!

Malcolm X bows. The auditorium's lights slowly fade to black. And his arm peels from its socket, dropping to the floor. Malcolm X walks backstage, followed by his crawling arm.

FADE UP:

INT. Theater—Movie screen.

Grainy, black-and-white World War II stock footage of a razed Eastern European city flickers on the movie screen. Plumes of smoke rise from the ruins. In undulating lines scratched directly on the film, grafitti of Mickey Mouse's head bob on the remainder of the city's standing walls. CORPSES, blobbed on the film's surface with black paint, litter the landscape.

> **BBC COMMENTATOR**
> *(v.o.)*
>
> Having armed and organized themselves into
> efficient paramilitary units in the second decade
> of the twenty-first century, the forces of white
> supremacy finally claimed victory in their war on
> the hordes of "lascivious mongrels" in the
> American homelands.

CUT TO:

A succession of propaganda posters modeled after the *Real Adventure* magazine covers of the 1950s. Drawn in the Disney house style, the posters feature distressed femmes fatales with large, projectile-shaped hooters and distended, bullet-shaped nipples captioned with recycled Nazi slurs lettered in German Gothic. Caricatures of sweating Blacks rip off Snow White's bodice and pinch her rosy nipples, a ring of Jews ejaculate jets of sperm on a fluttering Tinkerbell in competitive circle jerk, slit-eyed Asians sodomize Cinderella with a glass slipper and oily Hispanics gang-bang Sleeping Beauty.

Intercut with stock shots of a Gestapo raid on the Warsaw ghetto. The faces of the persecuted are blotted on the film stock with minstrel black, detailed with cartoonish eyes and lips. Mickey Mouse heads are scratched over the swastikas on the armbands of the Gestapo storm troopers. Signs are scratched in for fried chicken joints, liquor stores, storefront churches, check-cashing rooms, beauty parlors, barber shops, and Black Muslim mosques. The animated scratched lines of a swaggering B-boy with a boom box bops down the street. Musical notations dance from its speakers.

BBC COMMENTATOR
(v.o.)

> After a ruthless campaign of mass terror,
> brownshirt brutality, and outright assassination,
> the white supremacist armies won public
> sympathy to their cause by evoking the holy
> names of God and his only Son, claiming their
> actions were for the overall "White Christian
> good."

CUT TO:

Stock footage of the Nuremberg rallies in all their pageantry and zealous hysteria. The swastika-emblazoned flags, banners, and armbands, as well as all pictorial representations of Adolf Hitler, are masked on the film by vibrant, airbrushed images of Mickey Mouse with a halo sunburst effect. A dirge version of the *Mickey Mouse Club* theme song plays under the crowd's roars of "Sieg heil!" and "Yea, Mickey!" On close-ups of the actual Adolf Hitler, his face has been digitally reshaped by computer to resemble the world-famed rodent.

BBC COMMENTATOR
(v.o.)

> It was in this spirit of "white Christian goodness"
> that the Endlösung, or "Final Solution," was put
> into effect...

CUT TO:

Montage of Auschwitz-Birkenau death-camp atrocities. Atrocity upon atrocity is layered in explicit, stomach-turning detail, culminating in the final pyramid of bodies "clawing and mauling each other even in death" inside the camp's "delousing" chambers. The figures, again, are blotted over by blobs of minstrel black. End montage on crematorium door. Its sign reads:

FOR COLORED ONLY

Up Music: "When You Wish Upon a Star"

> **BBC COMMENTATOR**
> *(v.o.)*
> As in the words of that old Negro spiritual, the
> white man finally laid his burden down...

The crematorium's door swings open on whining hinges and a pile of ash and charred bone pours from the oven to the floor. A toothless skull crowns the ash mound. The title pops onscreen:

THE ROCKY-HORROR NEGRO SHOW

Music: Gothic speed metal.

Fade to black behind title. Roll credits.

Starring Hundreds of Dead Negroes

Fade music.

Fade up scorched ruins of New York City in long aerial shot. Manhattan's legendary skyline is obscured by voluminous clouds of black smoke. Lightning bolts flash at regular intervals. Slowly zoom in to rubble of blackened stone and melted steel.

>   BBC COMMENTATOR
>   (v.o.)
> The United States' Second Civil War in the
> twenty-first century had reduced the nation to a
> vast boneyard of ruinated cities and extirpated
> lives.

Wide shot of rubble-strewn terrain with an immense black cloud swirling in the background. The cloud flickers with an ominous underlight.

Camera up on FIVE "NEW WORLD" BLACK GUERRILLA SOLDIERS in ragged, blood-sopped uniforms. The THREE MEN and TWO WOMEN crawl from a heap of broken concrete and twisted steel, their hands ulcerated and blistered, their faces lined with exhaustion and defeat. The guerrillas run at a plodding pace, their arms dangling lifelessly at their sides. The swirling black cloud drifts closer and closer behind them.

ONE OF THE GUERRILLAS looks back. He screams. An enormous metal manta ray floats from within the swirling cloud. On its silver hull is a circled silhouette of a young black man crossed by a bold diagonal line.

A concentrated beam of heat shoots from the manta ray's beak. The guerrilla dissolves in the heat ray's backlight. His rags burn, his flesh melts, and his skeleton turns to ash.

Cross-fade to:

INT. Manta ray's observation deck—View screen—Day.

Wide aerial shot of Guerrilla Fighters in the crosshairs of the observation deck's view screen. A beam of light blasts the ragged band. They fry up gold and crispy, falling on the terrain like pieces of batter-dipped chicken.

The view screen buzzes and whistles and blinks with an assortment of colored lights. An imposing DEATH'S HEAD appears on the screen with the question:

ARE YOU READY FOR LEVEL THREE
OF LASER-FRIED COON?

Their fists balled around the view screen's joysticks, two small Mouseketeer-eared BOYS in rubberized flight suits with inflated ribbing come into view.

SPINNER

Bull's eye! Burned the wool right off his head!
Neat, huh?

CORKY

Yeah! And they look good enough to eat, too!

SPINNER

Eatin' niggers makes me fart! What's for dinner?

CORKY

Mom's makin' our favorite. Macaroni 'n' cheese!

SPINNER

Macaroni 'n' cheese! Yum, yum! That sounds like a bellyful of big fun! Let's go!

The two boys run off in excitement.

CORKY

Hope there's a mountain o' mashed 'taters!

CROSS-FADE:

INT. The Disney Magic Mall.

Bluebirds circle the spires of Sleeping Beauty Castle. A stylized yellow SUN with laugh-wrinkled eyes whistles in a cartoon sky. Musical symbols pop from its puckered lips. An elevated monorail hums through the caverns of the multi-leveled mall. The monorail stops and the two mouse-eared SPACEBOYS hop aboard.

Tilt down to MECHANICAL PUPPETS singing "It's a Small World" in a woodland campfire tableau. The freckled, rosy-cheeked, white-child puppets, in Naziesque Mickey Mouse uniforms, click their boot heels and fling straight-armed salutes around a naked, skewered, and trussed NEGRO roasting in the campfire's flames. A large red apple is lodged in his mouth.

BBC COMMENTATOR
(v.o.)

But far below the city's rubble was another world. A world blinded by fairy dust and cheap, sleight-of-hand tricks. A world populated by cantankerous ducks and talking mice. A world with holographic signs promising low, low prices and bargains galore. An underworld fun world for children of all ages. A live-in shopping world for the whole family. *A Disney World.*

CUT TO:

High-definition television screen in the spherical shapes of Mickey M's face. The screen crackles in a blizzard of snow,

97

static, and white noise, which recedes into a blip. The television broadcasts a picture of Sleeping Beauty Castle at night, a fireworks display bursting above its battlements.

Doe-eyed, busty, and swathed in leaves, TINKERBELL flutters onscreen in a trail of pixie dust, waving her wand. The U.S. Presidential Seal appears in a ring of radiant concentric circles, its eagle replaced by Mickey M's face. The ONSCREEN CAPTION reads:

A SPECIAL ANNOUNCEMENT BY
THE UNITED STATES PRESIDENT-FOR-LIFE

Tinkerbell grasps the folds of her translucent wings, curtsies, and flies away with the grace of a humming bird. Lose super of "Seal" and onscreen caption. Dolly in past screen for medium shot of castle.

The castle's drawbridge lowers across the moat with the rasp of rusted chains. A glass coffin slides from the mouth of the castle on a bed of dry ice. Its frosted lid creaks open. A MAN dressed in a conservative blue suit with icicles encasing his head like a ball of porcupine quills rises from the coffin. The prickled iceball turns to slush and falls away in chunks. The man smiles and clears his throat. The man is WALT DISNEY.

WALT DISNEY
Two score and twelve years ago, a great
marksman, in whose symbolic shadow we stand,
took aim, pulled the trigger, and shot a rabble-
rousing nigger. His shot rang out as a foreboding
death knell to millions of Negroes living happy as
hogs on the tax dollars of hardworking Christian
white folks like you and I.

"Uh-oh," they thought. "Dere go d'monthly
welfare check! Weeze gwine haf'ta go back ta
robbin' chickens fum d'hen house!"

But fifty years later, we rejoice in the marvelous fact that the Negro is no more. Fifty years later, we no longer suffer the indignified presence of "the blues" and "jellied pig-foot knuckles" that were the Negro's life. Fifty years later, we no longer hear the Negro complain he is "sadly crippled by the chains of discrimination," as he languishes on the urine-stenched street corners of American society, singing "doo-wop" and swilling from his jar of King Kong corn. Fifty years later, we no longer hear the Negro whine that he is "an exile in his own land" as he mounts our naive and trusting daughters, who offered up the golden down of their loins in an act of misguided compassion, impregnating her with his evil seed.

America found tranquility by laying the Negro to rest. We stripped him of his claim to humanity. We put down his revolt, which threatened to shake the very foundations of our nation.

I say to you today, my friends, through the miracle and power of imagination, I wished upon a star and made my dream come true.

I wished upon a star—

That one day this nation would rise up and live out the true meaning of its creed: "Hang the nigger and burn the Jew!"

I wished upon a star—

That one day in a wondrous shopping mall, beneath the red hills of Georgia, filled with rides and amusements for the whole family, the sons of former slave owners would dine on the sons of former slaves, secure in the knowledge their silverware was safe from theft.

I wished upon a star—

That one day the content of this nation would be judged by its lack of characters of color.

I wished upon a star—

And made my dream come true.

I wished upon a star—

That one day every Coon Town would burn to the ground, every Jig Stop and Cat Fish Row made low, the black places made white, up would be down, mice would talk, elephants would fly, the glory of Fantasy Land would be revealed, and all of Mickey's friends would see it together.

And when the hour of death knelled for the Negro, America became a nation of unsullied whiteness. Negroes burned on the prodigious hilltops of New Hampshire. Negroes burned on the mighty mountains of New York. Negroes burned on the heightening Alleghenies of Pennsylvania.

Negroes burned on the snowcapped Rockies of Colorado.

Negroes burned on every hill and molehole of Mississippi. On every mountainside, Negroes burned.

We let Negroes burn, and the stench filled every village and every hamlet, every state and every city, but we didn't care. In our hearts, we thought, "Let those Negroes burn!"

Then one day, the air cleared, and all of Mickey's friends, white men and white women, white boys and white girls, joined hands and sang, paraphrasing the words of that old darky spiritual:

"Gone at last! Gone at last! Thank God Almighty, them niggers is gone at last!"

100

INT. The Zombie Master's lair—Night.

With his conked head rolled back on his neck, the ZOMBIE MASTER sits in a canvas butterfly chair dressed in black, short-coated tuxedo with tails and a satin-lined cape.

His lair, located in an underground grotto miles below the Magic Mall's whimsical machinations, is decorated 1950s Pop Atomic with an Abstract Expressionist twist. Metal African masks, pared to geometric essentials, hang on the walls.

On a mouse-eared, wall-unit HD TV screen in the background, DOKTOR MENGELE DUCK, a monocled, Teutonic Donald in physician's whites, performs "wacky" organ-shifting experiments on BRER RABBIT, BRER FOX, and BRER BEAR. His assistants HUEY, DEWEY, and LOUIE whistle "Zippity Doo Dah" while they work.

Suddenly, the Zombie Master snaps upright in his chair. His gleaming pompadour is in spiked disarray. His gold-toothed grin is the sardonic smile of a clown in the throes of a methamphetamine rush. White lines spiral at furious speeds inside his dark-framed glasses' circular black fields.

THE ZOMBIE MASTER

I have seen the future! And I saw a Mau-Mau kissin'
Sannie Clause!

Slicked with greasy kid stuff, a duck-tailed HEAD pumps up and down in the Zombie Master's lap, its lumpy misshapen ass sparkling with sequins. The Zombie Master's pelvis bucks in orgasmic release and the spinning-eye Hypno-Specs fall off his face. His pupils expand to the size of quarters.

THE ZOMBIE MASTER

Buzzard elbows in chitlins à la king!

Green with mildew and pocked with worm holes, the duck-tailed CREATURE rises from the floor in sequined, ankle-baring bell-bottoms.

With its upper lip curled in an arrogant sneer and its cheeks swollen by a mouthful of congealed cum, the creature's pendulous belly rolls pass the flaps of its fringed, western shirt. It tugs at the lapels of its embroidered stand-up collar, nodding its head to an inner rockabilly beat. It swallows. And its Adam's apple bobs up and down.

The creature wipes a string of cum from its chin. The gob of cum falls to the floor, splashing the toe of its one blue suede shoe.

It should be evident by now that this bloated rockabilly beast is none other than that "Patron Saint of White Trash Trailer Parks"—the ELVIS ZOMBIE.

Standing, the Zombie Master pulls up his trousers, zips his fly, and adjusts his cummerbund. He embraces the Elvis Zombie, dancing the tango in orthopedic space shoes. Blue sparks leap from his eyes.

The Zombie Master sings:

THE ZOMBIE MASTER
I put a spell on you...!

Walt Disney reappears on the TV screen. The Zombie Master watches Walt with his brow furrowed in deep concentration. He lets the Elvis Zombie drop to the floor.

WALT DISNEY
Jubilation time is here again, friends! And I'm proud to announce our tenth annual "Second Coming of Christ" parade! This year is going to

102

be bigger and better than ever! There's gonna be
a parade on Main Street, USA, with floats 'n'
fireworks 'n' marching bands! We're gonna eat
lotsa corn dogs 'n' cotton candy 'n' sell balloons
'n' T-shirts 'n' "Wind Him Up and Watch Him
Walk Across the Water" toys! Come and see all
your cartoon friends act out your favorite scenes
from the New Testament! Goofy 'n' all the gang
will be there! And the best part is, *Christ won't
make a blessed cent!* Little hebe's been cleanin' up
for years, anyway! So come and join the fun! It's
gonna be spectacular! Heck, I might even
resurrect myself for the occasion!

The Zombie Master shakes his head, eyeing Walt Disney with
disgust.

THE ZOMBIE MASTER

There's somethin' wrong with you! Somethin'
missin' someplace somewhere! Bellevue! That's it!
You ain't all there! You look like—ummm-umm—
I don't know!

The Zombie Master hurries from his lair, followed by the
limping Elvis Zombie.

FADE

INT. The Zombie Master's Laboratory—Night.

The laboratory, paneled in sheet metal and stocked with human body parts turned blue with frost, is an enormous walk-in refrigerator dominated by two growling Grafenberg generators flaring tines of electricity. CADAVERS of both genders and all races lie in naked decay on operating tables throughout the room. Hundreds of arms and legs hang overhead. Several faces stitched in catgut are scattered across a butcher-block tabletop. Racks of headless torsos without arms or legs are stacked against the walls. Glass jars of eyes, noses, and ears floating in pickling brine are shelved alongside rows of half-pint bottles labeled "Alligator Wine."

J.F.K.'S HEAD, complete with exit wounds, scuttles across the floor on spindly spider legs, chasing a centipede-appendaged PENIS.

J.F.K.
I always wanted to suck my own cock!

Trailed by the Elvis Zombie, the Zombie Master strides into the laboratory with his cape billowing behind him. His brow is stern with determination. His breath is white in the chilled air. With a wooden oar, he stirs a stew of eyeballs bubbling in a cauldron of purple liquids.

THE ZOMBIE MASTER
Take the blind out of an alligator.
Take the left eye out of a fish.
Take the skin off of a frog. And
Mix it all up in a dish.

104

With his arms whirling in high-speed motion, as if he's suddenly grown octopus tentacles, the Zombie Master stitches and sews, reconstructing the roomful of cadavers. He reanimates each of the cadavers with a sip of Alligator Wine.

Squinting, the Zombie Master holds a petri dish up to the glaring overhead light.

THE ZOMBIE MASTER

In this dish, I have saved the tissue trimmed from the nose of Captain Nee-Gro, that 3-D wonder of the white man's technology. And with it, I plan to clone his proboscis back to its original Negroid proportions, placing it in the service of the *revolution!*

Tilting a half-pint bottle of Alligator Wine to his lips, the Zombie Master grumbles—

THE ZOMBIE MASTER

Baboon-fuckin' muthafucka don't know nuthin' 'bout no eight-bar blues! Nigga need to go back to school and learn his ABC's and 1-2-3's so he can put some blues back in his Do Re Mi!

He sets to work. There is an explosive sneeze. Droplets of lime-colored slime fleck his face. He stares up in awe.

THE ZOMBIE MASTER
(grinning)
LOOK OUT WHYTEY! MICHAEL'S GONNA GIT CHO' MAMA!

EXT. Disney Magic Mall—Day.

Mickey Mouse smiles like a benevolent Big Brother in a colorful flower arrangement of the National Socialist flag on the Magic Mall's great lawn. Perched in the trees of an adjacent grove, a flock of MECHANICAL ZOOT-SUITED CROWS caw high-spirited gospel songs, shake their tail feathers, and jangley tambourines. A portly CLERIC-COLLARED CROW exclaims in a leathery voice:

CLERIC CROW
Chirren! Git ready to cakewalk to *Hebben!*

EXT.—Main Street, USA—Day.

The whistling cartoon sun shines with summertime brilliance on the parade of nymphet-fresh blond MAJORETTES, who, under the shade of brightly fringed, pom-pom parasols held aloft by blackfaced, buck-dancing DANDIES, kick young, tanned legs and gold-tassled boots in the air, exposing their clean, white panties. The muddy blare of a brass MARCHING BAND is heard offscreen.

With flags unfurled, synchronized MICKEY YOUTH MARCHING BAND MEMBERS, attired in lederhosen and mouse-eared leather caps, goose-step past festive crowds of crucifix-worshiping, corn-dog-chewing CAUCASIANS who look and act like an extended family of inbred Appalachian mutants gathered for a Fourth of July picnic. As the first float rolls into view, the CROWD roars—

HONKIE-MUTANT CROWD
Heil Mickey! *Heil Mickey* CHRIST!

Crowned by a circle of thorns, Mickey Christ hangs by his inflated white-gloved hands on a neon-lit cross with his owlish Walter Kean eyes staring sadly at the sky.

Hook-beaked MYNAH BIRDS, in black rabbinical wear, hurl rocks at the CRUCIFIED RODENT. A YARMULKED BIRD peeps under Mickey's loincloth—

YARMULKED MYNAH BIRD
(thick Yiddish accent)
Circumsize? What's to circumsize?

In a mock manger rolling on a set of fatwheel tires, a haloed Huey, Dewy, and Louie tweak one another's beaks in a wicker bassinet. The MAD HATTER and his TEA-PARTY PALS reinterpret the Last Supper. The crowd titters with affectionate laughter.

Thunder booms and lightning cracks across a gold-streaked, purple sky.

With puffed, rose-tinted cheeks, pudgy pink CHERUBIM blowing long golden trumpets flap above the gayly bannered, turn-of-the-century street, heralding the arrival of a surfer-blond JESUS with plastic, flickering eyes. The crowd whistles and applauds.

With a white-feathered dove roosting on his shoulder, OUR LORD OF THE PLASTIC FLICKER EYES stands barefoot on a purple-cushioned throne, smiling like a fluffy young girl crowned Queen of the Rose Bowl Parade. He lifts his arms to the sky, gesturing as if he were about to bless the crowd. A red-petaled rose appears between his fingers. His fingers pop and smoke like a string of Chinese firecrackers. The rose transforms into many loaves of Wonder Bread and cans of Bumble Bee tuna fish. Jesus hurls them at the crowd.

To the delight of his tuna-fish and Wonder Bread—fed following, Jesus sits down on his throne and swaps jokes with the HOLY GHOST.

107

HOLY GHOST

Guilt! You idiot! *Guilt!* I said drive the *guilt* out of the temples!

SFX: An explosive, offscreen sneeze.

JESUS CHRIST

God bless you!

Jesus turns his head in the direction of the sneeze and is doused in slime. His flickering plastic eyes blink in cartoon amazement.

EXT. Sleeping Beauty Castle—Day.

A gigantic cherry-shaped NOSE, looking as if it were dipped in a crock of chocolate fondue, cleaves to the sides of Sleeping Beauty Castle. A green paste leaks from its nostrils.

EXT. Main Street, USA—Day.

The Crowd scrambles in blind panic, slipping and sliding in the muck slaking the sidewalks.

EXT. Sleeping Beauty Castle—Day.

Slithering down the castle's walls, the GIANT SNOTBOX excretes a trail of slime, honking and snorting its way toward Main Street, USA.

With a mighty sneeze, the GODZILLA-SIZED PROBOSCIS erupts like a lava-spewing volcano, slathering the streets in a thick carpet of mucus. Brown boulder-sized boogers tumble down the street, crushing panicked pedestrians in their path. Flailing BODIES drown in the flood of green goo. The Nose rears up in rage and snorts with cyclonic force. PEOPLE are spirited off the ground, twirling into the hairy darkness of its twin nose-holes.

Suddenly, the street splits into a web of cracks. The Christ float jostles like a rickety carnival ride. Chunks of tar and concrete are belched into the air. Hundreds of SKELETAL HANDS grapple their way through the debris and tear at the float's painted crusts of papier-mâché, exposing the float's chicken-wire frame.

Swarms of Zombies climb from the crater beneath the float with entrails hanging in ropy loops from their stomachs' rotted recesses. Oozing a putrid puree of pukesome pus, hundreds of Zombies claw up the sides of the float, and a pustulated hand reaches out to OUR LORD. The hand yanks out one of his eyes. The eyeball is mashed into the bowl of a hash pipe and smoked. Another of the Zombies bites his finger, siphons the blood into an empty bottle of Thunderbird wine, and drinks it. Christ's rib cage is ripped from his chest, dunked in a tub of hot sauce and butter, then barbequed in a bonfire. His head is twisted from his neck, then eaten like a slice of watermelon.

The Disney Magic Mall is overrun with Zombies, who shamble through the ice-cream-and-candy splendor of Fantasyland and ride the Monorail over the technological wonders of Tomorrowland.

As Zombies spin inside oversized teacups, dissolve to:

INT. Sleeping Beauty Castle—Day.

A hand-held lantern throws the shadows of the Zombie Master and the limping Elvis Zombie against the walls of the cramped, cobwebbed corridor. The Elvis Zombie carries a stake and a wooden mallet.

THE ZOMBIE MASTER

It is time to end Disney's reign of whyte-
supremacist terror!

ELVIS ZOMBIE

Yes, master. *Kill whytey!*

A BAT flies into view. The Elvis Zombie catches it by its wings
in midflap and gobbles it whole, smearing his face with rabid
blood.

DISSOLVE TO:

INT. Sleeping Beauty Castle—Subbasement.

The Zombie Master with his lantern and the Elvis Zombie
with the stake and mallet stand at the top of a long staircase
of crumbling stone. They walk down the stairs.

The Zombie Master opens the metal door of a refrigeration
chamber. Inside, Walt Disney rests in his glass coffin.

The Zombie Master stares down at the sleeping Walt, lifting
the coffin's glass lid. He takes the stake and mallet from the
Elvis Zombie and hammers the stake into Walt's heart.

Smoke and sparks sizzle from Disney's neck. The hollows of
his eyes burn bright blue. His body flops like a landed fish.
His face contorts into a series of unnatural expressions.

The Zombie Master's eyes are wide with realization.

THE ZOMBIE MASTER

Why Disney ain't froze at all! He jus' a puppet in
his own mad design!

Disney's face blackens and melts. Underneath is a network of circuitry wire and tiny blinking lights.

WALT DISNEY

Elephants would fly...fifty years later...and...swill...from his jar of...urine-stenched street corners...and the glory of Fantasyland would be revealed!

Walt's eyes flash and his head blows up. His body flares into flames.

FADE

EXT. Main Street, USA—Evening.

With his chest puffed in victory, the Zombie Master strides down Main Street, USA. His assistant limps at his side. The Disney Magic Mall has been reduced to rubble. Fires burn everywhere. The streets are clogged with mucus. Hundreds of Zombies wander about, munching bloody body parts. GOOFY's head grins on top of a tall wooden stake. Blood drips from his eyes.

The two stroll past a Majorette trapped in a bubble of snot, stepping over a white dove squashed in the mud. A Zombie in the Mad Hatter's "10/6" top hat shares a crack pipe with the hookah-toking CATERPILLAR. The ABRAHAM LINCOLN ROBOT stumbles about in confusion.

Finally, the Zombie Master and the Elvis Zombie come upon the Giant Nose. Blood pours from its nostrils in great profusion. Sadly, it is dying in the street. The Zombie Master has tears in his eyes.

THE ZOMBIE MASTER

Friend, you're a good soldier. You fought with valiancy and courage. The Revolution will not forget you.

Ragged Zombies stagger out of the burning rumble and gather around in great numbers. The Zombie Master pats the Nose.

THE ZOMBIE MASTER

Good-bye, my friend.

The Elvis Zombie's eyes are turned heavenward, nearby flames light his face. He croons a gospel song. The other zombies moan behind him.

ELVIS ZOMBIE

Mosin' on up to Moses on a mule...

The music swells and the song takes a sudden, upbeat, rock-and-roll turn.

ELVIS ZOMBIE

One for the money! Two for the show! Three to get ready! Now *go! Go! Go!*

With a complicated series of karate kicks and jabs, the Elvis Zombie moves like he's just returned to the Vegas stage. Unfortunately, as a result of advanced decomposition, his body parts fly straight into the lens of the camera. The spider-legged J.F.K. head croaks beside the dung heap we knew as "Elvis."

As the end credits roll, everyone holds hands around the bleeding nose in a "We Are the World" tableau. A feathered SKELETON painted with psychedelic sixties designs plays an electric guitar. The skeleton bites the strings and sets the guitar on fire. The following words apear:

THE END

INT. Grindhouse—Auditorium—Night.

As a worn velvet curtain slides over the white space of the movie screen, the auditorium's lights brighten overhead, and Bubbles dives underneath the row of theater seats bolted to the floor in front of her.

Crawling on her belly toward the outer lobby, Bubbles wades through puddles of warm malt liquor and soggy french fries, watching the ongoing scene out of the corner of her eye.

Bouncing in unison with the coiled spring of a Slinky, a boisterous mob of MUPPET B-BOYS swagger down the aisles on the toes of their unlaced sneakered feet, swinging cotton-stuffed arms in stylized arrogance.

With siren-whining boom boxes blaring behind them, two ball-capped Black Muppets, or BUPPETS, in T-shirts declaring, "IT'S A DICK THAANG! YOU WOULDN'T UNDERSTAND," share a plaid cardboard boat of fried chicken wings slathered in hot sauce.

FIRST BUPPET

Boyee! I got a stupid fresh concept! Let's beam up on the rock, go to Central Park, *an' rape us some whyte women!*

SECOND BUPPET

Yeah! Get our picture on th' front page of th'*New York Post,* shakin' hands wit' d'fat Reverend Do Rag—"YOUNG NEGROES SCAM MUCH BOOTY IN CENTRAL PARK!" Scare mo'fuckas on d'six o'clock news. *Shit be dope*!

113

FIRST BUPPET

Word! Den we do a rap, mash th'shit on wax, an' make us much money! *Catch all th' honeys!*

SECOND BUPPET

Yeah! Dat's d'trick! *Have all d'babes suckin' our dicks!*

With splintered chicken bones scattering in all directions, the two Buppets jump up and down like a pair of caged rhesus monkeys on crack. Swelling to monstrous proportions, they then roll on the floor, hammering hambone rhythms on their heads; each looks like two large Easter eggs with enormous erections.

SECOND BUPPET stands. His cotton hands gesture in excitement.

SECOND BUPPET

Peep dis', Money! *We film th'shit! We film th'shit!* Right there! In the park! As it happens! *Cinema verité*. Claim th'shit was a revolutionary act jus' like that brutha wrote back in th'sixties!

FIRST BUPPET
(rolling confused Ping-Pong-ball eyes)
What brutha in th'sixties?

SECOND BUPPET
(smacking first Buppet on the back of the head)
Th'brutha what designed th'pants with th'dick stickin' out, knucklehead! We screen th'shit at Cannes, win us a Palm D'Or, an' get our dicks sucked by a bevy of flybabes in bikinis on th' Riviera!

114

FIRST BUPPET

I heard that! Then we could open up our own
"joint" an' sell ball caps an' T-shirts with *actual
photos* of us bangin' th'bitches in the bushes!

SECOND BUPPET

Word! Who knows how far we could go? We might
even sell sneakers on TV! But t'git our shit off
the ground, we first gots to cop th'rock!

First Buppet speaks to a MAN seated offscreen whose shadow
is thrown against the floor.

FIRST BUPPET

Yo, man! You got five dollars?

The Shadow stands.

SHADOW
(cheerful)

You want five dollars? Sure. I'll give you five
dollars—*here!*

SFX: *Blam-blam!*

A blue flash illuminates the intersecting circles of surprise
on the face of the FIRST BUPPET. Cotton filling falls in
clustered yellow clumps from the bullet hole torn in his chest.
Plush toy intestines plop from his split gut.

SHADOW
(concerned)

Are you sure that's all you need? I know times are
tough. Let me give you *more.*

SFX: *Blam-blam.*

The bullets pop the Buppet's painted Ping-Pong-ball eyes. A pink pincushion brain drops from his crumbling papier mâché skull.

> **SHADOW**
> (*brightly*)
> As the drug crisis facing today's young African-Americans in the inner cities reaches genocidal proportions, I'd be more than happy to do my share and help out. Think a ten spot'll hold you until you get on your feet?

SFX: *Blam-blam!*

First Buppet topples to the floor. The shadow turns to the Second Buppet.

> **SHADOW**
> (*friendly*)
> How 'bout you, pal? You look like you could use a few bucks.

> **SECOND BUPPET**
> *No man! That's okay! Keep yo' money!*

> **SHADOW**
> (*compassionate*)
> No, take it. *Really.* It's alright. I've got plenty. More people in my position of privilege should do as I do! You'll be able to go out and buy yourself that brand-new pair of sneakers I saw advertised on TV by that paragon of black enterprise!

SFX: *Blam-blam!*

Second Buppet pops like a rubber balloon. Cotton ticking clouds the air.

The shadow fires his gun at random, popping Buppets as if downing duck silhouettes in a carnival shooting arcade. Gangs of screaming, gold-toothed Buppets stampede toward the exits, trampling one another underfoot.

Shattering the overhead bulbs in a fusillade of Uzi fire, a posse of armed Buppets plunges the theater into a state of disordered darkness; the Shadow's narrow white face is reflected in the firefight's stroboscopic light.

In white-laced Dr. Martens, the Shadow sings and dances on a goggle-eyed heap of COTTON COON CORPSES. He is accompanied by gunfire, police sirens, and belching, beat-box Buppets.

SHADOW
Don't forget Thom Dixon!
He warned about race mixin'!
But the Liberals slipped their tricks in!
And the Niggers got their kicks in!
Shovin' their big black dicks in!
Remember Sammy huggin' Nixon?

Fight for your right to be White.
(Don't accept the tripe!)

I only echo your fears
The White Race/the Higher Man
Will disappear!

Time is getting shorter
In this world of chaos and disorder.
It's like breathing under water.
Look at the shrinking White Race border.
White People! Pledge loyalty to the Order!

Fight for your right to be White.
(Don't accept the tripe!)

Niggers armed with Uzis
Paid for by Zionist Jewsies

117

Fuckin' nigger floozies! Gonna
Whack you while you snoozy! Then
Piss in your Jacuzzi!

I say we need a dramatic new mathematic
To subtract this mongrel static!

"*Number One: Sight your target. Become like a reptile. He said it*
with a smile. And his eyes were bright. You lay out your pattern of fire
from left to right."*

Mulatto zombies, mixed up
Commies and piebald geeks!
Let's get together and waste
All those weak-blood *freaks!*

"*I intended to kill them. You decide what's right and wrong.*"*

Burrheads! Baboons!
'Gator bait! Coons!
Round 'em up! *Blast 'em!*
Ship 'em to the moon!

Fight for your right to be White!
(Don't accept the tripe!)

"*If your brain is a glass globe inside that skull, you work on reflex,*
you work on reflex. His exact words were: 'Give me five dollars.' The
bulge in my pocket…is not a threat to me."*

SHADOW

Suckin' germs from
Green monkey sperm!
Bustin' baboon butt
In a jungle hut!

---

*The videotaped confession of a noted subway gunman.

118

Yo! Hunkie! Purebred
And funky! Don't get yer
Blood mixed up with that
Deadly monkey the Afro-
American junkie!

Fight for your right to be White.
(Don't accept the tripe.)

"*If I had more bullets I would have shot them again and again. My problem was I ran out of bullets.*"*

White people, wake up!
The government of Zog
Has your minds
In a fog!

The Shadow opens his black trench coat. A girdle of dynamite is strapped to his chest. He lights the fuse.

Boom!!!

One dead white boy.

CUT TO:

INT. Grindhouse—Lobby—Night.

Night of the Swinging Nightsticks

The explosion's impact slams Bubbles through a set of double doors, sending her tumbling over the lifeless body of a Buppet sprawled in a pile of popcorn and cotton balls on the floor of the outer lobby. She relieves the Buppet of its ball cap and Uzi, leans against the popcorn popper's cracked glass case, and pulls herself to her feet. She adjusts the cap on her head, twisting its bill to the side.

A Buppet staggers out of the men's room with a crack pipe pinched between his gold-capped teeth and notes that her nipples protrude through her torn bikini top. He fondles the bulge in his crotch.

BUPPET
(grinning)
Yo', AAP* girl, I got *big* monkey meat for you!

Bubbles balances the Uzi on her hip. She aims for his throat.

BUBBLES
You're as square as your haircut, chump.

She pulls the trigger. The Buppet's head pops from its neck in a spout of cotton balls and hums through the air in a whir of bleeding colors. Crashing through the lobby's plate-glass window, the head spins out into the night.

---

*Anglo-American Princess.

EXT. Grindhouse—42nd Street—Night.

The head whirls into a mob of Buppets running amok under the grindhouse's neon-fringed marquee, falling into unwitting black cotton hands. The severed head's eyes circle inside their sockets. The Buppet holding the head shrieks in fright. His fluorescent bristles flare and stand on end.

FLARE-HAIRED BUPPET

YOWSAH—! I been hit by th'Hip-Hop hoodoo!

The frightened Buppet flings its arms in the air, hurling the head through the window of a Korean electronics shop. Glass rains to the sidewalk in glittering shards.

As bullets zip all around, gangs of bottle-throwing Buppets rampage in the midst of raging bonfires and overturned garbage cans.

A phalanx of police officers parade in military formation along 42nd Street, tossing vapor-spewing tear-gas canisters into the riotous mob.

Truncheon-wielding police officers armored in insectoid riot gear gallop on dark, demon-eyed steeds, nogging knots of POP-EYED NIGS.

Sirens wail. Bubbletops spin. Cop choppers hover overhead.

Bubbles steps through the grindhouse's empty window frame, belching incandescent Uzi burps in the greenish fog, and battles her way through the maze of battered bodies bleeding cotton balls on the blacktop. Buppets burst into flame and disintegrate in daffy dervish dance.

A metallic, drumlike jungle beat clanks through the streets with ominous reverberations. An opaque shadow blankets the crowd. Confusion turns to still life. Tension stiffens the air.

121

Suddenly, a bat-winged wad of iridescence drops from the sky and gobs the squad of MOUNTED POLICE. Plastic pop-ball eyes look up in hung-jawed awe.

CUT TO: A FIVE-HUNDRED-FOOT-TALL CYBORG towers over the stark neon glare of Times Square.

It looks like a cross between a *Tyrannosaurus rex* and a steel-drivin' John Henry with a retractable chrome-capped penis gripped in its pincer claw. The cyborg's face is flat and brutish, with two red beams glowing from inside the sockets of its ovoid head. Tiny rockets built into its massive black frame breathe jets of blue flame. The cyborg walks with halting steps. Its footfalls are loud and leaden. Its eyes flash danger red.

The cyborg strokes its segmented metal hose, spurting a semen-like substance through the air, and a deluge of jellied jism pours through the streets. Buppets scatter in terror. Police officers are squashed underfoot.

CUT TO:

With infrared, cybernetic night vision, the cyborg scans its surroundings. A frost of crystallized cum coats all in its path. A cursor beeps on the cyborg's heat-sensitive optical monitor. And alien glyphs are generated in digital display. The monitor magnifies the image of a rubber-clad dominatrix with an enema tube coiled around her arm.

Looking below the glass-encased poster of the dominatrix, the cyborg's head tilts with a grinding whine, finding Bubbles crouched in the shadows of a porn-theater's open-air foyer.

Scooping her up in its claw, the cyborg stares at her quizzically, the light in its eyes softening with what appears to be affection. Its jaw snaps open.

Bubbles is tossed inside. *Crunch*!

INT. Cyborg—the Image Chamber.

Negromancer

Screaming at the top of her lungs, Bubbles tumbles through the tunnels of the cyborg's twisted plumbing and lands on the octagonal floor of a black-lit room with a pastiche of ever changing imagery on its walls. She sits up and stares in confusion.

As her eyes adjust to the ultraviolet light, she sees a blurred, backlit Silhouette shuffle from the image chamber's walls. An empty white linen SUIT slowly walks into focus. The suit's pant legs jerk like a marionette's, and a pair of white gloves hovers below its sleeves. Lavender-colored vapors swell from the opening in the neck of its shirt collar and condense into a floating mass of glow-in-the-dark dreads. Two luminous eyes and a plump, red mouth glow in the ovoid space under the nest of knotted hair.

TALKING DREADS

Do you like my little toy? It's the Negro of the future—*one hundred and ninety tons of urban combat machinery.* My designers were inspired by a book written at the turn of one of your Earth centuries: *Tom Swift and His Steam-Powered Negro.*

An aged hardback volume materializes in midair. The TALK-ING DREADS' white-gloved hands open the book and point to an engraved illustration of a husky, broad-shouldered white boy shoveling coal into a chute located at the rear of a huge Black robot. Its caption reads: *"Why, Tom, it'll rival the cotton gin!"*

123

Charming illustration, isn't it?

The book is tossed aside. It evaporates in a shimmer of lavender glitter. Bubbles tilts her head in curiosity and stares into the pair of suspended eyes. The mouth knowingly smiles.

TALKING DREADS

I seem familiar to you, don't I? There's something about my face you know, you can't place it, but you know it, and you find your familiarity with it strange. You shouldn't. I've made contact with your world before.

My first attempt at intelligent communication with this planet was a disaster, a real misfire. I communicated my presence to a receptor, a Scottish woman living in India, by projecting myself into her dreams. Unfortunately, she garbled my transmission. The image skewed in her mind, rooted, and spread like a weed. This was the result.

A second illustrated volume appears, this time in a radiant burst of magenta. The Talking Dreads hands the book to Bubbles, who opens it and reads:

Lil' Black Zambo

Lil' Black Zambo was a little nigger boy. Or pickaninny. Or jigaboo. Or any number of names we have for little colored children—shine, smoke, snowball, dinge, dust, inky, eggplant, and chocolate moonpie. And since Lil' Black Zambo lived with his mammy in a one-room hut made of mud and leaves near a croc-infested swamp in the Jungle, we can call him 'gator bait, too.

There was not much in the hut where Zambo and his mammy lived: a dirt floor, several pairs of dice (Zambo and his mammy liked to roll the bones), and hundreds of big, brown cockroaches with wings snapping *clickity-click splat* as they buzzed through the hut and slapped against the walls.

Zambo's pappy, Tambo, who liked to drink cheap coconut wine, ran off long before Zambo was born, so Zambo and his mammy were very, very poor. They didn't give out welfare checks in the Jungle. The Jungle was uncivilized. Or at least that's what Zambo's mammy, Mambo, said. "When we gwine git civilized so I can git on d'welfare?"

Zambo's mammy was as big as a gorilla and looked like one, too. She had big, red lips stretched out of shape by two clay plates stuck in her face and a big, white bone pushed through her nose. Her knuckles even dragged on the ground.

Zambo was no looker himself. "Lawd! What I do to deserve such an ugly chil'?" his mammy moaned. "An' why you give him such *nappy* hair? It look like d'wool knotted up on a sheep's ass!"

Zambo was real, real black. *Spear-chucker chocolate,* his mammy said. She clacked her lips and told Zambo he d'darkest chil' she ever seen. Darker than her frying pan even.

"Dat pretty damn *dark!*" Zambo said.

"*Damn right!*" Mammy exclaimed. "When you born, you so dark, d'docta slapped me!"

Zambo's eyes grew big and sad when his mammy said that, thinking, "What I do to be so black an' blue?"

(Sometimes Louie Armstrong flew out to the Jungle with his band and jammed for the Jungle Bunnies. That's where Lil' Black Zambo picked up all his blues references. All the Jungle Bunnies in the Jungle would show up, dressed in their finest feathers, and smoked the Mezz. As Pops blew, the Jungle Bunnies, high as a kite, cheered, "Oooga-booga!"*)

Now Lil' Black Zambo loved to eat watermelons. He didn't eat the red juicy part because he didn't like the seeds.

"What I look like sittin' in d'Jungle spittin' a bunch o' seeds?" he said. "Can't kill no lions wif a moufful o' seeds!"

So he ate the rind and threw the rest away.

But more than watermelon, Zambo loved pancakes. He loved pancakes more than he loved his saucer-lipped mammy. Mile-high stacks of pancakes dripping with sweet sugary syrup and lots and lots of hot yellow butter. Zambo's lips got greasy just thinking about it. *Umm-umm!*

Zambo's mammy made him pancakes three times a day, every day. She made her pancakes from scratch. They didn't have Aunt Jemima in the Jungle.

Zambo liked missionary sausage with his pancakes real special. "Mammy, when we gwine eat mo' Bible-totin' whyte folks?"

So Zambo's mammy would file her teeth, streak her face with fresh daubs of paint, and go into the bush, trapping herself a nice, plump white missionary. She'd grind him into wormy bits of red meat, stuff him into a tube of monkey's intestines, and fry him up grease-poppin' brown.

"Uuuumm-yum, Mammy! I *love* whyte people!"

One day, as Zambo's mammy stirred pancake batter made from scratch, and battled an airborne squadron of flying cockroaches, she complained:

"We so uncivilized! We don't have welfare checks or Aunt Jemima mix or nuffin in d'Jungle! When we gwine git civilized an' go pick cotton fo' d'rich whyte folks in America?"

Zambo tugged at the fringes of his mammy's straw skirt. (Zambo's mammy wore a straw skirt and nothing

*Editor's Note: "That nigga can play his ass off!"

126

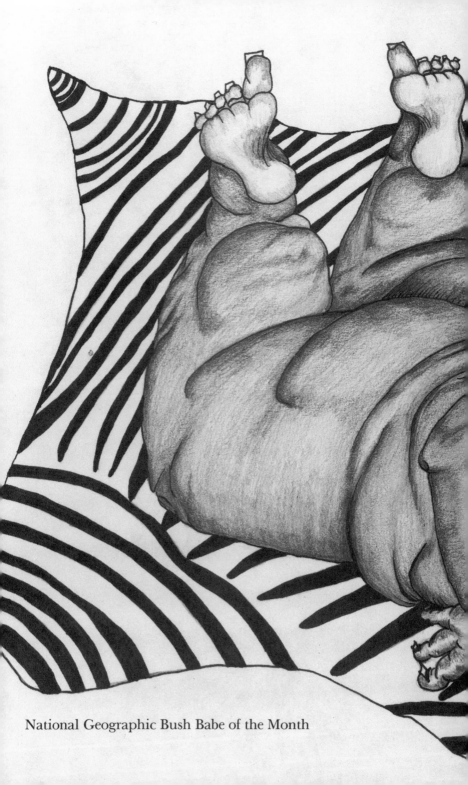

National Geographic Bush Babe of the Month

more. When her picture was published in *National Geographic*, baring her black bushbabe bod and flat Jungle Woman tits, she knew she'd finally been civilized. She could just see the welfare checks flying in.) "An' not only dat, Mammy!" he said. "We ain't got no hot yellow butter, neither!"

"Oh no!" his mammy wailed. "We ain't got no hot yellow butter! What me an' my poor chil' gwine do now? He gone haf t'eat his pancakes wif sweet sugary syrup! Damn dis uncivilized Jungle life!"

With her face buried in her hands, she dropped to her knees on the hut's dirt floor and began to cry.

"Don't cry, Mammy!" Zambo said, forking a pancake into his mouth. "Look! I eatin' it! It good wif jus' d'sweet sugary syrup! I don't need no old hot yellow butter! Hot yellow butter ain't good fo' you no way! It high in cholesterol, it harden on yo' arteries, an' give you hypertension, d'number-one killer o' black folks today! Dat one thing I'll say fo' dese damn flyin' cockroaches. Dey strict vegetarians!"

As was the habit of his kind, Zambo was lying.

While his mammy howled like a horse-whipped hound, Zambo took his plate of pancakes and marched from the hut with a pout. He was in a huff.

"Shoot! I'm gone git me some hot yellow butter! Sittin' 'round whinin' fo' d'rich whyte folks t'come civilize us pickin' cotton wif Aunt Jemima an' welfare checks ain't gone git me no hot yellow butter! What cotton anyway? Shoot!"

Zambo walked through deep, dark jungle with the pancakes stacked high on his plate. Suddenly, a Tiger sprang out from behind a coconut tree. "Hey boy! Can't you read the sign? It says, *no darkies allowed!*"

"No," said Zambo. "I can't read. I ain't been civilized. What's a 'darkie'?"

"Don't talk smart at me, boy!" said the Tiger. "We eat little darkies like you where I come from!"

"*You does?*" Zambo trembled, his eyes wide with fear.

"Yes. I 'does,'" said the Tiger with considerable condescension. "Like *hell* you does!" Zambo zipped to the top of the coconut tree, trailing a plume of dust.

The Tiger was confounded by the little nigger boy's speed.

"You sneaky little burrhead! Come down here this instant!"

Zambo stared down at the Tiger from the top of the coconut tree with the plate of pancakes balanced on his lap. He looked like a lump of coal.

"Is you out yo' rat mind? Does you think I'm gonna climb down there jus' 'cause you say so? An' let you eat me, too? Dis might be d'Jungle, Mr. Tiger, but my mammy didn't raise no fool!"

Zambo's grin displayed a set of perfectly white teeth.

The Tiger's face turned red with frustration. He stomped his paws and thrashed his tail.

"You insolent little ragoon!" the Tiger fumed. "We give you people all the mud and leaves you need for your roach-infested huts, plenty of open space to chuck your spears, all the monkeys and coconuts you can eat, and all I ask for in return is one lousy meal! Is this how you people show your gratitude?"

"What 'graptitude,' Mr. Tiger?" Zambo asked innocently.

The Tiger grew blind with rage at Zambo's nig-gerheadedness. He rolled his paw into a ball and shook it at the sky.

"Just one woolhead little Jungle Bunny! That's all I asked for! One kinky-haired little ink spot! Who's going to miss him? His big, ugly, bone-through-the-nose, gorilla-lookin' mammy? Not that fat, funky, watermelon and pancake eatin' bitch! She done lost her mind and don't know *that's* gone yet!"

That made Zambo mad. The tiger was talking about his mammy! She might be big, black, and ugly with a bone through her nose but she was *his* mammy. What was wrong with that Tiger? Didn't he have enough sense to know you didn't go around talking about other

128

people's mammies like they were pellets of monkey doo-doo?

"You talkin' junk now, sucka!" said Zambo. "Don't lemme haf t'come down there an' beat th'stripes off yo' butt!"

The Tiger laughed. "I'll slap the black out of you and that fat flapjack freak you live with! Now what you got to say to that, *punk?*"

Zambo hit the Tiger in the head with a coconut.

The coconut raised a big, throbbing lump between the Tiger's ears. He staggered around the coconut tree with a circle of stars revolving around his head. Birds chirped *tweet-tweet.* An asteroid flashed past his eyes.

Upon recovery, the Tiger angrily shook his balled paw at Lil' Black Zambo.

"I'm gonna put a hurtin' on you now, you Uzi-armed little crackhead! When I get through with you, you'll never listen to rap music again!"

The Tiger began running in circles around the coconut tree.

"I hope you enjoy the view up there, boy, 'cause when I get my claws in you, you gonna be a *dead* nigger with an attitude!"

The Tiger ran faster and faster and faster. He ran so fast he looked like a yellow ring of swiftly spinning light.

"*Burrhead!*" the Tiger roared. "*Jungle bunny! Ink spot!*"

The Tiger ran faster still. "*Spear-chucker! Mau-mau lips!*"

Suddenly, there was the gleam of flame and the acrid smell of smoke. The glare hurt Zambo's eyes. In an instant the Tiger was gone. Lil' Black Zambo blinked in amazement.

He couldn't believe what his eyes had just seen. He rubbed them with his tiny fists and blinked again. It was true. The Tiger had vanished.

And directly below him, in a bright puddle circling the foot of the coconut tree, was seven-hundred pounds of hot yellow butter.

Lil' Black Zambo smacked his lips.

His last thought, just before he shimmied down the trunk of the coconut tree, was how he'd like, with his pancakes, to sink his freshly filed teeth into a string of sizzling missionary sausage.

THE END

Closing the book, Bubbles discovers the Talking Dreads pacing the octagonal floor with the agitation of a caged panther.

TALKING DREADS

That's how my image filtered back into your world. Nothing in this woman's frame of cultural reference allowed for any comprehension of my presence in her psyche. She couldn't imagine the existence of things outside her sum of knowledge. She resorted to what she knew—puckish dark-skinned boys and authoritarian tigers—to explain the confusion caused by my presence. If it had been otherwise, she would've experienced a mystical conversion of untold depth, and been deemed a prophet in your world.

I didn't anticipate the cumulative results of this woman's confusion. In fact, I was startled. I was appearing in storybooks, comic strips, and animated *cartoons!* My face adorned bags of flour, postcards, bottles of molasses, bed sheets, and rolls of wallpaper! I was even given to children as a windup, spring-action *tin toy!*

Though my intelligence is superior to the best minds on earth, I didn't understand it. I'm an extraterrestrial being, not an all-purpose *cosmic Sambo!* I come from another planet! I have

130

technological capabilities your world won't realize for at least another two thousand years! You don't waste that kind of potential by reducing it to a graphic on a box of *bleach!*

Of course, I made attempts to rectify the situation. One transmission, the very same message I broadcast to the woman in India, in fact, was intercepted by a psychiatrist, who gave your world a work entitled *Peau Noire, Masques Blancs,* or *Black Skin, White Masks.*

Once, I tap-danced in the dreams of a filmmaker known for animating urban animal fables of a pornographic nature. I sang to him in a whisper, *"I'm a nigger man. Watch me dance."*

My most successful try was with a musician who named himself after an Egyptian deity. He proved to be an excellent receptor. Eventually, though, he began leading an orchestra of drug-addled horn players through his arrangements of "Let's Go Fly a Kite" and "Zippity Doo Dah." It was then I realized it was all quite futile and gave up on the idea. Intelligent communication is not a quality your world is known for in this or any other galaxy. Instead, I've decided to take over your planet and treat you like the cattle you are.

As Bubbles considers the gravity of the Talking Dreads' decision, he dissolves into a blurred, lavender-colored mist, his suit crumpling into a limp pile on the floor.

The mist wafts toward the ceiling and molds into a human-oid oval, inflating to enormous size. A disembodied, dread-locked head bobs in the air with Tenniel's vanishing Cheshire Cat grin.

TALKING DREADS

Yes, Ms. Brazil, the *Cosmic Sambo* has plans for the degenerate whyte man...

The Talking Dreads' white-gloved hands bookend the words:

THE ULTIMATE PLAN FOR THE
DEGENERATE WHITE MAN

The walls of the image chamber spin with light and color, projecting a holographic mirage of a small rural town in midair suspension.

Circled by a nimbus of phosphorescent murk, the Talking Dreads' disembodied head speaks in a smug, no-nonsense voice.

> **TALKING DREADS**
>
> On the surface, "Garvey's Corner" is a town as typical and serene as any other on the golden plains of America's wheat belt.

CUT TO:

Dawn. The sun rises over the small midwestern town of Garvey's Corner. A wizened BLACK MAN in blue denim overalls pushes a junk cart strung with clanging pots and pans. He drums his wares with two metal spoons, calling out in bluesy singsong.

> **JUNK MAN**
>
> Rags! Old iron!
> *Raaags!* And
> Old iron!

The JUNK MAN rolls his cart past the war hero's statue erected in the town square, his song echoing in the alleys. An American flag undulates in the morning breeze. A handbill blown through the streets is caught in the grate of a curbside gutter. It reads:

TOWN BAR-B-Q TONITE!
COME ONE! COME ALL!

With its circa 1920s architecture, Garvey's Corner is the town
that Norman Rockwell and his brother George might have
built for their boyhood train set. In a well-ordered, tree-
laden product of municipal planning stands a town hall, a
post office, a church, a little red schoolhouse, a sheriff's
office, and a train depot. It's a town so staunchly American
and small town in its values and thinking it could be called
the Town That Made Frank Capra Throw Up! Portly SHOP-
KEEPERS open the doors to their stores. The gray-haired
SCHOOL MARM climbs the steps to the schoolhouse. The
postman waves good-day to the depot's STATIONMASTER. The
SHERIFF chats with the junkman.

SHERIFF

You're sure you got enough horse sense to
understand what I'm sayin' to you now, Joe?

The Junk Man whinnies and stomps his foot. The Sheriff
pats the old man's bald, black pate, flipping the OLD MAN a
sugar cube. The Junk Man intercepts it with his tongue.

SHERIFF

I like it when you use your tongue like that.
You're quick as a bullfrog, Joe, and a real credit
to your kind.

TALKING DREADS
(*v.o.*)

A town where the air is sweetened by the warm
aroma of a hot apple pie cooling in the window of
a humble white frame house.

133

EXT.—One-Family House—Backyard—Morning.

Crouching beneath the open back window, TWO FRECKLE-FACED BOYS steal a deep-dish apple pie from the windowsill.

TALKING DREADS
(v.o.)
It's the kind of town where grizzled menfolk sit around the pickle barrel in the general store and hack gobs of chewing tobacco into the brine of phlegm-filled spittoons, cracking off-color jokes about their swarthy, sweat-secreting hired help.

EXT.—General Store—Late Morning.

FIRST MAN
That there's a luger.

SECOND MAN
Yup.

FIRST MAN
Big, red, slimy sucker.

SECOND MAN
Yup.

FIRST MAN

Looks like a squid.

SECOND MAN

Yup.

FIRST MAN

Figger we can sell it to the dagos?

SECOND MAN

Yup.

FIRST MAN

Taste real good to 'em, too. Fry it up with garlic, be real tasty.

SECOND MAN

Yup.

FIRST MAN

Make a great pizza topping.

SECOND MAN

Yup.

FIRST MAN

Make a fortune off them wetbacks.

SECOND MAN

Yup.

FIRST MAN

Niggers, too.

SECOND MAN

Yup.

FIRST MAN

...

SECOND MAN

Starin' at that sucker makes me kinda hungry.

TALKING DREADS
(v.o.)

It's a town where busty blond girls and square-jawed boys tool down Main Street, USA, in souped-up jalopies, jitterbug to big-band swing, and drink nothing stronger than bottled pop in the local malt shoppe.

EXT.—Main Street—High noon.

A pudgy-faced, gap-toothed, tousled-haired TEEN behind the steering wheel of a sputtering roadster turns to the big-busted, pale-haired GIRL beside him:

BOY

Say, Judy, howsabout drivin' over to the bad part

136

of town* so you can give me a blowjob in the back
seat?

JUDY

Neatto, Andy!

INT.—Back Seat of Andy's Car—Bad Part of Garvey's
Corner—Midafternoon.

JUDY puffs her cheeks and blows a stream of air on the
smegma-webbed projectile pulsing in ANDY's lap.

ANDY

Gee, Judy, this is *swell!* Can I come in your
mouth?

TALKING DREADS
(v.o.)

Garvey's Corner is the kind of old-fashioned
American town that still knows the value of a
day's hard work, the colors of its country's flag,
and the Lord's commandments.

EXT.—Outskirts of Garvey's Corner—Late Afternoon.

As the sun sinks below the horizon, the TOWNSPEOPLE march
to the edge of town armed with hoes, pickaxes, coils of rope,
and an American flag. The TOWN PASTOR leads the parade

---

*A residential area dominated by plaster madonnas and the thick, oily
smell of fried garlic

with a gold-crossed, leather-bound Bible clutched to his heart, his eyes aimed piously at the sky.

Suddenly, in a billowing trail of dust, the Junk Man zips ahead of the pack, zooming past the sign

NIGGER! DON'T LET THE SUN SET!

EXT.—Town Square—Dusk.

A bonfire blazes. The townspeople, convened at the war statute, dab their tearing eyes, their hearts swollen with reverential emotion. Just below the American flag, swinging sadly at the end of an oiled rope, is the Junk Man's tarred corpse with the "TOWN BAR-B-Q" handbill pinned to his flannel shirt.

> **TALKING DREADS**
> *(v.o.)*
>
> But surfaces are deceiving. What looks like the
> familiar stars and stripes of Old Glory's true red,
> white, and blue is, in reality...

The American flag smokes into flames. The Junk Man raises his head, opens his eyes, and laughs maniacally. A ripple shivers across the surface of the holographic mirage. A black, red, and green flag flies above a bronze statue of Marcus Garvey.

> **TALKING DREADS**
> *(v.o.)*
>
> ...the black, red, and green flag of the Black One
> World Government! Or *Sambo's World!*

The CITIZENS of Garvey's Corner aren't crying at all. They are wiping off a peach-colored veneer of greasepaint because, underneath the grease, each inhabitant of Garvey's Corner is *black!*

TALKING DREADS
(v.o.)

For underneath its folksy charm, Garvey's Corner is as phony as a set on a Hollywood back lot!

Garvey's Corner microscopes to toy dimensions.

Firebombed buildings, rubble-strewn lots, storefront churches, and iron-grated liquor stores encircle the "town's" false facades. DESPERATE PEOPLE mill in the streets. A trio of stingy-brimmed COOLIES croon doo-wop under the billboard

WELCOME TO SAMBO'S WORLD!

TALKING DREADS
(v.o.)

Located at the heart of America's most dangerous slum, Garvey's Corner is a mock town where blacks are trained to *look, act,* and *think* like ordinary law-abiding white citizens in order to undermine all the rights and freedoms American society has to offer the white race without the slightest detection!

These agents of subversion are so expert in the chameleon's art of camouflage they can even mimic the actual smell of whites by bathing in tubs of *rancid milk!*

Outlandish you say? A plot too farfetched for the average Negro mind to conceive? Stop a moment and *think.*

Have you ever felt personally embarrassed for someone who couldn't dance? I mean someone

139

who *really* couldn't cut the carpet? And you, the very embodiment of style, fashion, and attitude, groaned that this goldfish-gobbling jackass in the raccoon coat is the reason why the white race has such a bad name in discotheques throughout the world? *Think again!*

That person was probably born and raised in Harlem—*trained to make white people look bad!*

INT.—The Sambo Institute for Artificial Caucasians ("White Today for a Black Tomorrow")—Classroom—Night.

A TALL, ELEGANT BLACK MAN in floor-length white robe and a knit skull-cap stands at the blackboard.

> **INSTRUCTOR**
>
> Remember, class, Minister Louis Farrakhan once remarked, "You can make a whyte man out of a black man, but you can't make a black man out of a whyte man," so we made a whyte man out of Louis Farrakhan and got...

The video image of FRED MACMURRAY'S DOPPELGÄNGER flickers on a television monitor. The Doppelgänger peels the rubber prosthetic mask from its face. And LOUIS FARRAKHAN crocodile smiles from under the tufts of cotton and Band-Aid-colored latex. With a stick of white chalk, the instructor writes on the blackboard:

FRED "FARRAKHAN" MACMURRAY:
THE FLUBBERIZED NUBIAN MAN

> **INSTRUCTOR**
>
> If we are to successfully subvert the soul of the whyte man and dominate the globe with our negritude, we must inhabit his being as if it were

140

our own! We must think as he thinks! See as he sees! We must attack his mind, undermine his "will to whiteness," and defeat him before the battle's begun! In other words, *we must drive the whyte man crazy!*

Tearing the rubber prosthetic from his face, the Instructor, too, looks like Fred MacMurray.

CUT TO:

INT.—Image Chamber.

A pinwheel of black and white lines spins in darkness. With an eerie electrical hum, the Talking Dreads' pinpoint pupils incandesce and expand in size. His words visibly vibrate from his mouth in squiggling phosphorescent circles.

TALKING DREADS

Whites are often, quite literally, *blind* to the physical presence of blacks. It's as if a melanin bomb discharged in the unconscious of the white race and destroyed the whole of the world's black population. Blacks have become an unseen entity in the distorted landscape of the white psyche. An absence. A *void.* We are now a race of *invisibles.*

As the Talking Dread's vocal emanations orbit her head and dissipate into rings of smoke, Bubbles sinks into a deep hypnotic sleep. The soft evening song of crickets can be heard chirping from a suburban lawn.

TALKING DREADS

As invisibles, our work becomes the subliminal work of sorcerers. We must steal into the last sanctuary, the sanctuary of dreams, and attack that portion of the brain that understands not

141

words, but images. We must burrow into the blind spots of personality, chanting the black incantations of our otherworldly ancestors, and change the signposts of slumber...

CUT TO:

INT.—Bubbles' Brain.

A sudden brilliance of blinding intensity bursts behind Bubbles' lids. The light wanes in afterglow. And an ovoid HEAD, ruffled with flakes of peeling black paint, looms in grainy obscurity.

The head turns with a rusted scrape. A tiny lantern swings before its unblinking eyes. A duck-billed cap sits on its frizz of iron curls. Its nose is flat and flared with a pair of protruding sausage-shaped lips. Its canary-yellow teeth snap open and closed.

The jodhpured JOCKEY chugs like a pistoned engine gathering steam, lurching with metal clanks. With creaking mechanical movements, its thigh-high riding boots gleaming in its lantern's circle of light, the jockey marches past a tract of identical ranch-style houses.

His IRON HOMEBOYS fall in line.

Organized in single-file formation, with backs inclined, elbows crooked, and little iron feet clanging, the ARMY OF COON-FACED LAWN ORNAMENTS trot in synchronized two-step up the lamp-lit street.

Cacophonic music blares in the air. A coal-skinned IMP hovers at the rear, tootling Moondoc's "March of the Iron Lawn Jockeys" on its soprano saxophone.

FADE

Shelter From Negro Fallout

A committee of the National Academy of Sciences, in a recent study of national preparedness for the fallout of volatile Negroes, concluded: "Adequate *shielding* is the only effective means of protection."

A PUBLICATION OF THE OFFICE OF CIVIL AND DEFENSE MOBILIZATION

Introduction

Let's take a close hard look at a dark fact in American life. The Negro is a walking, talking time bomb set to explode without notice at any moment. It could happen anywhere. At any time.

Imagine yourself in the lobby of a high-rise office building in the midtown section of Manhattan. You have an important business meeting to attend. You check your watch. You have time to kill. So you get your shoes shined by a rag-popping, rheumy-eyed old Negro with a pint of Jack Daniels stuffed in his back pocket.

He looks friendly enough. So you share some jokes. Exchange ball scores. Admire his rag's syncopated rhythm. Discuss the size of Mike Tyson's neck.

The Negro turns, squats, and buffs your shoes with his buttocks. *"What rhythm!"* you enthuse. *"If only my wife could shake like that!"*

Without warning, a column of flame shoots to the ceiling and a shower of cinders blackens the air. The next thing you know, the rag-popper is gone, you're coughing a lungful of incinerated Negro, and, worst of all, your skin has turned completely black! *Permanently.*

143

It could happen. Anywhere. At any time.

And the consequences are far more serious than a few combusted bootblacks. The fallout from the exploding Negro's darkening melanin agents could infect millions of innocent Caucasian men, women, and children close to the point of ground zero, reducing this country to a nation of lumbering Al Jolsons in mammy-whining blackface.

Think of the confusion it would create at the country club. No one would know *who* to send through the service entrance!

The United States federal government has a shelter policy based on the knowledge that most citizens beyond an exploding negro's range of blast will survive if they have adequate protection from Negro fallout. A shelter incorporates the fundamentals of Negro fallout protection—shielding mass, ventilation, and space to live. Shelters offer protection not only from the fallout of exploding Negroes, but from boiling Jews, frying Puerto Ricans, and other ethnic undesirables as well.

Remember—protection must be provided *before*, not after, the sirens sound!

What is an exploding Negro?

For that matter, what's a Negro? The word sounds like an encrusted growth bubbling with milky poisons on the reproductive organs of an aged streetwalker. I hear the word Negro and my penis shrivels.

Contrary to our whimsical folklore, the Negro didn't sprout full-grown in the cotton fields of the South, moaning some spooky-sounding spiritual (though that stuff on their heads would lead one to suspect otherwise). In fact, the idea of the Negro has been with us much longer than Negroes themselves. We need only turn to that tome of truth and wisdom, the King James Bible, which says, in rich word and apt metaphor, blackness is *disease, death, damnation,* and *despair,* as well as basic sin and evil, to understand that the first Negro was Satan. This is why Negroes are born with horns and barbed tails. And why Africa is so hot.

144

Unfortunately, the diabolical origin of the Negro's anatomical peculiarities doesn't explain the nubbed condition of James Brown's even browner teeth.

Now, we know, for the Bible implies it so, that the Negro is Satan, a word that originated among the ancient Hebrews. Negroes, therefore, are an invention of the *Jews!*

Barney Brimstone
Director
Office of Civil and Defense Mobilization

FADE UP:

INT.—Suburban Home—Living Room.

TELEVISION

Farina one o' dem homey, pig-tail-eatin', no-pussy-
gettin' kinda niggas. His mouf be ashy. He a'ways
be barefoot wif his thumbs hooked in d'staps o'
dem Farmer Brown overalls, complainin' 'bout
how he can't get hissef no pussy. I tol' da nigga
his bref stink! If you stop eatin' them pigtails, you
might get yourself som' pussy!

Hiccuping, high-pitched laughter enlivens the gloom of the
suburban living room. Light wavers across the faces of
grimacing, black, iron-orbed LAWN JOCKEYS camped in front
of a television set. An animated, circle-based figure of
BUCKWEE capers on the screen, rolling his white pop-ball eyes
and flapping his hotdog-bun lips.

CARTOON BUCKWEE

You eat so many goddamned pig tails you got da
muthafuckas growin' out yo' head! If you wasn't
so country, wif all dem pigtails you got, you could
say you was Ziggy Marley an' get you some pussy!
In all kinda colors!

The LAWN JOCKEYS scramble through the house as the
television broadcasts in the background, scrawling grafitti
on the walls.

CARTOON BUCKWEE

Eat to live, live to eat, brutha! Elijah Muhammad
didn't eat no pig tails, but he ate plenty o' pussy!

146

Dat's why Malcolm left da Nation! 'Cause da
Messenger was snackin' back on carrot cake and'
pussy pie!

After stealing meat cleavers and serrated knives from the
kitchen drawers, the army of little iron men marches up the
stairs. Moondoc's music blares.

The Lawn Jockeys barge into a room, throwing elongated
shadows against the wall. An ELDERLY WHITE COUPLE with
masked eyes sleeps blissfully in bed.

The couple awakens, heads swiveling in blind confusion.
The Jockeys grin.

And the blades come falling down.

INT.—Image Chamber.

Close-up on Talking Dread's phosphorescent face.

TALKING DREADS

You could wake up one morning with lips the size
of two country sausages, an inability to pull a
fine-tooth comb through your hair, and an
inexplicable craving for deep-fried pork by-
products slathered in vinegar and hot sauce.

The Talking Dreads points directly into the camera as a
montage of white faces spins around his head. While he
speaks, each face turns *black*.

TALKING DREADS

Yes! This could happen to you! You! You! Or even
YOU!

CUT TO:

Bubbles in blackface with a big Pebbles Fintstone dinosaur bone pushed through her coils of blond, lint-flecked hair. An oval of ash frames her mouth.

> **BUBBLES**
>
> I may file my teeth, have a big bone through my nose, and wear a plate in my lips, but *I am somebody!*

SMASH CUT TO:

INT.—Bubbles' Brain.

Bubbles—with her limbs stretched in the cross-barred figure of the double Vesuvius man—tumbles inside a circle of revolving NEGRO FACES. The Negroes, in late 1940s dress, are convulsed in laughter.

> **BUBBLES**
> *(v.o.)*
>
> I sank deeper and deeper into the maelstrom of my own mind, whirling in a vortex of improbable visions until, finally, I was transported to the scene of a forgotten childhood game.

Bubbles fades into outlined transluscence and disappears.

The ring of cackling coons rotates around a nymphetic NINE-YEAR-OLD, nude, with dusty peach-colored skin, demonic lynxlike eyes, and a froth of dazzling blond curls. She lounges in blissful languor on a rumple of blankets spread across a heart-shaped bed.

> **BUBBLES**
> *(v.o.)*
>
> As a child, my parents treated me like a glorified house pet. I was their golden flower, their

blossom of blond innocence. In their eyes, I
embodied the very essence of uncorrupted purity.

Dozens of dolls dangle overhead, their faces disfigured
masses of hardened black bubbles. Plastic limbs and eyeballs
twirl on the ends of colored strings.

BUBBLES
(v.o.)

I resented this. And took it out on my dolls. I
would pluck out their eyes, shove their faces on
the stove, and watch their hair flare in a sparkle
of pungent flame.

Moist red paint gleams on the Nymphet's pouting, plum-red
mouth. Pink buds button the low hillocks of her chest. Red
stiletto heels accentuate the line of her coltish, reedlike legs.

BUBBLES
(v.o.)

So, in spite of my parents' pampering, or possibly
because of it, I was the kind of bright-eyed
moppet who enjoyed playing with her powdered
panties down.

The Nymphet's crimson-tipped fingers furiously flick the
rose-tinted crease of her hairless, hymen-sealed pudenda.
The wheel of circling Negroes shatters in a whirl of shards.

BUBBLES
(v.o.)

At first, I confined my games to the bathtub,
turning its faucet until it gushed full force
between my legs. Then, gradually, my games
grew more complex.

With the upper half of her face hidden behind a black, bird-
winged mask, another naked GIRL-CHILD stumbles into the

149

room wearing bubble-toed shoes with high platform heels and a feathered, wide-brimmed fedora.

THE SCARLET NYMPHET

Where you be gettin' them *fly* threads, Blackbird?

The WHITE CHILD in the bird-winged mask slaps the Scarlet Nympet across the mouth. A thunder crack resounds throughout the room.

BLACKBIRD

Later for my habadasher, *bitch!* Where be my
money! You know my dick don't be gettin' hard
until I be gettin' my money!

THE SCARLET NYMPHET

Boo-hoo-hoo! Don't be beatin' on me, Blackbird! I
already done be down on d'stroll an' sol' me
plenty o' plump, pink pee-hole!

Tight shot on NYMPHET's eyes. The corners crinkle in mischief.

BUBBLES
(v.o.)

Sly and rebellious, with a keen eye for the street,
I was a city kid. A *New York* city kid. I was not
unlike those unmanageable little girls who,
crossing the line dividing the wealth of the Upper
East Side from the poverty of Spanish Harlem,
played stink finger with little Puerto Rican boys
in housing-project hallways.

DISSOLVE TO:

INT.—42nd Street Grindhouse—Day.

In leotard, tutu, and Wayfarer shades, the Scarlet Nymphet sits in a darkened movie house surrounded by loud DRUNKS and dozing DRUG ADDICTS. The lights of the movie screen flicker on the Nymphet's face.

BUBBLES
(v.o.)

I'd duck dance class, sneak into rundown Times Square movie houses in my leotard and tutu, and catch classic inner-city entertainment.

The Scarlet Nymphet snaps her fingers and wiggles her behind in the theater seat.

THE SCARLET NYMPHET

Git it, Sweetback! Give it to me *good,* daddy!

Movie images of MELVIN VAN PEEBLES balling a WHITE BIKER DYKE are reflected on the surfaces of the Nymphet's shades.

BUBBLES
(v.o.)

I laughed at Blackenstein's four-cornered 'fro, which presages the cubed coifs of Hip-Hop.

CUT TO:

Film clip of a BLACK FRANKENSTEIN MONSTER in a suit with oversized shoulders slanting at odd angles. A column of squarely cut hair sprays straight up from his head. Wearing gold chains and unlaced Air Jordan chimney-sweep boots, the Monster dances with arthritic stiffness, grunting an incoherent rap song into a microphone.

151

What makes a whyte man? A combo of CAT, RAT, *and* DAWG!

BUBBLES
(*v.o.*)

I sat in thrall to the black power pussy plays of
Foxy Brown and Cleopatra Jones.

CUT TO:

Trailer of the Scarlet Nymphet in a Day-Glo, butt-huggin'
micro-miniskirt and a big, bulbous Afro wig, leaping
through the air with a flying kung-fu kick. She topples a
gang of thugs, spraying them with machine-gun fire. Seven-
ties disco-funk crackles on the scratchy soundtrack. Bold
titles burn across the screen—

SEE: "THE HARLEM HARLOT"!
SHE BAAD! SHE BLACK! SHE BEAT MUCH BUTT!
HER NAME IS BUBBLES BRAZIL!
AND SHE GOT A *BIG* AFRO!

The Scarlet Nymphet's bubble of kinky hair grows bigger.
And bigger. And *bigger.*

BUBBLES
(*v.o.*)

And I once wondered why a werewolf would wear
dreadlocks.

CUT TO:

Film clip of WEREWOLF with black, red, and green dreadlocks
growing in the middle of his face.

By day, he praised the glories of Jah. But at night—the full moon brought out the *Beast of Babylon!*

Blinded by his suffocating tangle of hair, the werewolf runs into walls and stumbles over garbage cans.

THE RASTAFARIAN WEREWOLF OF WATTS!

BUBBLES
(v.o.)

But it was a triple bill featuring the lewd likes of Rudy Ray Moore that inspired my version of the Coon Game.

CUT TO:

Film clips from *Dolemite, The Human Tornado,* and *The Monkey Hustle.*

BUBBLES
(v.o.)

I first learned the Coon Game from my grandfather, "Big Bellies" Brazil, who slapped on the shoe polish and played it in the thirties, when the Chicago of *Amos and Andy* darkened the airwaves of American radio.

CUT TO:

Nineteen-thirties art card of white suburban family settled in their living room, awed by the emanations from their cathedral radio. Each face is a clownish, white-lipped mask of black greasepaint.

BUBBLES
(v.o.)

And he learned it from his grandfather, "Even
Bigger Bellies" Brazil, who toured the country in
corkface and said, "Unless Othello shot craps, ate
watermelon, and cut Desdemona with a razor,
playin' niggers paid better than Shakespeare and
got bigger laughs."

CUT TO:

Grainy, sepia footage of blackface MINSTREL reciting Shakespeare in butchered black dialect through mouthfuls of
watermelon.

BUBBLES
(v.o.)

"Big Bellies" said blackface was the cornerstone of
American independence. Without it, we might
not have ever thrown that shipment of tea to the
bottom of Boston Harbor and we'd still be a
colony of Britain today.

CUT TO:

Black-and-white footage of potbellied, cigar-chomping
blackfaced "INDIANS" in crow-feathered bowlers and buck-
skin pants, waving straight razors at frightened ENGLISH
SEAMEN.

BUBBLES
(v.o.)

"Big Bellies" also hurled baseballs at the heads of
niggers seated on the plank of the amusement
park's Dunk the Darky concession and slipped
strings of lit firecrackers into the back pockets of

154

unsuspecting spooks. As their pants popped into flame, he'd ask, *"Who farted?"*

CUT TO:

Baseballs careening off the head of a BLACK MAN. His eye is swollen shut, his lower lip is puffed, and his nose is broken.

BUBBLES
(v.o.)

Laughing at niggers is our first great national pasttime. "If we didn't laugh at niggers," "Big Bellies" said, "we wouldn't have known what to do with vaudeville or radio or movies or T.V. We wouldn't have known whose picture to put on the pancake box." Laughing at niggers is at the root of popular American entertainment.

CUT TO:

Montage condensing the 1959 television documentary on the Nation of Islam, *The Hate That Hate Produced,* sweetened with sitcom laugh-track.

BUBBLES
(v.o.)

So I took the Coon Game and turned it into a masturbating minstrel show. That's how my friends and I learned life's funky facts. When my friends came over to play, I'd break out the bootblack, and say, *Let's get dirty!* And we'd act like a bunch of drunken niggers in a down-home honky-tonk on Saturday night.

DISSOLVE TO:

INT.—Upper Westside Brownstone—Living Room—Day.

A naked, SHIRLEY TEMPLE–CURLED LITTLE GIRL in blackface shouts to a group of naked, blackface PREPUBESCENTS.

SHIRLEY TEMPLE–CURLED LITTLE GIRL

Hey everybody! Throw yo' *ass* in the air like you don't care! And do THE UNCLE REMUS!

The LITTLE GIRLS' wiry black limps twitch in a spastic combination of camp sixties dance steps, as they bump behinds with a lewd, rude, and crude attitude.

BUBBLES
(v.o.)

We'd get *low down*—wobblin' our knees in a bowlegged chicken dance, shakin' an' twitchin' an' rollin' our hands all over our young behinds *real* nasty.

Leaning over the surface of a glass-topped coffee table, the group of naked little girls snort lines of chocolate-colored heroin. The Shirley Temple–Curled Little Girl boasts—

SHIRLEY TEMPLE–CURLED LITTLE GIRL

My daddy shot smack with *Bird!*

BUBBLES
(v.o.)

We smoked up my parents' expensive Hawaiian reefer, stole booze from their liquor cabinet, listened to James Brown at chandelier-shaking volume, finger-fucked in my bedroom, and laughed at Richard Pryor on the VCR.

INT.—Upper Westside Brownstone—Bedroom—Day.

The Scarlet Nymphet pets with the Shirley Temple–Curled Little Girl on the heart-shaped bed. James Brown screams and sweats on the screen of the TV set.

BUBBLES
(v.o.)

Who else was I gonna laugh at? Amos 'n' Andy were dead.

As James Brown sings "Make It Funky," his face contorts into a frightful leer.

BUBBLES
(v.o.)

But, in our minds, we weren't the culprits. How could we be? Those weren't *our* faces. Those weren't *our* bodies. We would never put our mouths *down there!* We were *white* and *well-bred.*

It was those *black children* from the welfare projects! They did it! Those moon-headed, Kool-Aid-drinking, doo-doo-colored *Tar babies* in ragamuffin hand-me-downs!

They smoked the reefer! *They* stole the booze! It was *niggers!* Not us! *Niggers!* It was *niggers* poking their greasy, fried-chicken-pickin' fingers into our *wet, underaged pussies!* Not us! *Niggers!*

The Shirley Temple–Curled Little Girl straddles the Scarlet

Nymphet and rubs the glistening halves of her painted black ass in the Scarlet Nymphet's ecstatic face. Her rectum dilates.

SHIRLEY TEMPLE–CURLED LITTLE GIRL

Throw yo' ass in the air like you don't care!

And a moist, corn-studded turd spills from her ruffled hole. The turd slides into the Scarlet Nymphet's puckered mouth, smearing across her lips soft and fudgy.

James Brown grins and sweats on the TV set.

INT.—Image chamber.

Bubbles rubs her clitoris in agitation as she regains consciousness.

The ever-changing symmetries of the Cyborg's floor dissolve like crystals of frosty window breath and fade to glass transparency. Blighted cityscapes travel at blurred velocities below Bubbles' feet.

The Talking Dreads decelerates speed.

Coasting above the city's rooftops, the Cyborg's floor magnifies Manhattan in detail, surveying semen-spattered buildings frondescent with reeds, vines, palms, and dense tropical undergrowth.

Bubbles swoons in a spell of stomach-dropping vertigo.

A swell of VOMIT cascades from her mouth in a fan of Day-Glo fluorescence. It scuttles into a corner—green and crab-legged with round, tentacled eyes.

Grinning, the Talking Dreads bends over and lifts the multi-legged Vomitoid into his arms. He strokes the creature with affection.

TALKING DREADS

Your company has been most amusing, Ms.
Brazil, but I'm afraid it's time for you to go.

Smiling amicably, the Talking Dreads' eyes flash with silver light. And Bubbles disappears in a cloud of vapors.

Poof!

EXT.—Harlem Skies—Day.

The Cyborg fades into the sunlit horizon. Bubbles falls fast and far—

                    BUBBLES
                    W
                    h
                    a
                    t

                    a
                    m

                    I

                    g
                    o
                    n
                    n
                    a

                    d
                    o

                    .

                    .

                    .

—and plunges into the feculent waters of the Harlem River.

Splash!

INT.—Harlem River.

160

As a school of harelipped FISH with phosphorescent scales nibbles clusters of floating feces, Bubbles sinks through the river's hazy brown waters with her jacket billowing in a wreath above her head. Muffled words pop from her mouth in a cloud of rising air bubbles.

BUBBLES

...in this stinking *shitpool?!*

Bubbles' behind bounces on the river bottom, finally landing on a carpet of rotted jellyfish. Wincing with disgust, she peels the mucusy clumps from her rump, averting her eyes in distaste.

Suddenly, her eyeballs distend in horror. Air bubbles spume from her throat in a burble of muted screams. Her uvula swings from side to side.

Encircled by a wall of rusted automobiles standing upright in the mud, the ragged CORPSE OF A PIMP flaps in the polluted currents like a scarecrow in an evening breeze, its feet encased in cement, a gold tooth gleaming in its ravaged skull.

Adrenalized by fear, Bubbles swims through the murk with the motions of a bullfrog, colliding with the CORPSE OF A WELFARE MOTHER seated on the stoop of a sunken brownstone. The corpse topples on impact. Bubbles splatters in the mud.

As the corpse's bloated husk sinks into the soft, dark silt, with a brightly capped crack vial in the fist of its swollen hand, Bubbles slowly rises through the water toward the surface of the river.

In her ascent, she floats past a brood of ringworm-stricken BLACK CHILDREN sitting in rigid death pose on the brownstone's stairs. Clothed only in "TEENAGE MUTANT RASTA ROACH" T-shirts, the children hold glass-stemmed crack pipes between their lips, gazing absently with bloodshot Walter Keene eyes.

161

Bubbles sails by an unanchored subway car adrift in the rivers' excremental silence. Rotund CHEFS in puffed plug hats and aproned kitchen whites stand motionless in the subway's windows, holding porcelain plates stacked high with buttered pancakes.

A shark-finned sedan with bulbous chrome bumpers floats aimlessly in the distance. Impeded by a congealed clump of remaindered paperbacks, Bubbles swims in the sedan's direction, slogging her way through the soggy, shit-stained pulp of *The System of Dante's Hell*. Suddenly, the sedan rockets through the water at demon speed, churning up a backwash of foam and feces.

Bubbles flips out of its path. The sedan whirls clockwise in the water and again plows in her direction. Zomboid CRACKHEADS man the wheel.

With the sedan on her tail, Bubbles heads for the brownstone and disappears through its doorway. The sedan crashes into the stoop, crushing the corpses on the stairs. The mangled remains float away in bloated chunks.

Bubbles drifts into the hall, through schools of phosphorescent fish, and swims toward the stairwell. When her fingers reach the railing, she pulls herself hand over hand up the stairs, her body floating in horizontal extension.

At the top of the stairs, Bubbles wades in the water of the second floor's door-lined corridor.

On the floor below, the sedanload of zombied B-BOYS slog into the brownstone and trudge toward the stairs in clumsy Frankenstein slo-mo.

A pork-bellied WHITE MAN in traditional Quaker wear floats through an open door on the second floor, his eyes shining with the hard glitter of fool's gold. His knees are bent as if knelt in prayer, and his arms are stretched in front of him. His hands hang limp in the water.

162

With a chain of dung orbiting him, the Quaker Man drifts in Bubbles' direction. Clusters of laugh bubbles pop from his mouth.

Bubbles turns to escape. But barnacled B-Boys block the stairs.

Circling the Quaker Man with quick and nimble movements, Bubbles darts through the water and shoves open the nearest door.

She swims into the room.

Inside, fragments of a blood-stained mirror are scattered on the floor. A pair of pouty lips are painted on the wall. A table is caked with candle wax. And hundreds of obscene chocolate figurines swirl in the water's diarrhetic hues.

Bubbled laughter burbles behind her. Bubbles twirls around to face the source of the sound.

The Quaker Man bobs in the doorway, his dead rodent hands hanging before him. His laughter shakes his lumpy, white face like a small sack of potatoes, his mouth springing open and closed like a wooden dummy.

The Quaker Man's face foams in the water like crystals of bromide, dissolving into a froth the color of diluted milk.

Dead rodent hands wipe away the grayish film.

Luminous, psychotic eyes stare back at Bubbles.

Familiar psychotic eyes in a familiar black face. The familiar black face of the family Maid.

As the Maid grins, baring her canary-yellow teeth, Bubbles turns her head in horror and stares down at the floor.

BUBBLES
(*v.o.*)
Fading from one world into another, my

163

surroundings melted like Dali's watches in a sandblown dreamscape.

Upon seeing her reflection multiplied in the fragments of mirror, Bubbles pops into a wisp of ghostly invisibility.

INT.—Brownstone—Upper Westside Manhattan—Bedroom—Dawn.

EXTREME CLOSE-UP ON:

With serpentine ribbons of smoke curling from its hot, orange embers, a joint is cradled in the groove of an ashtray's rim. It is the color of beach-bleached bone and looks like a mummified cock stained by a ring of red lipstick.

> **BUBBLES**
> *(v.o.)*
>
> When I first gazed at my reflection in the
> bedroom mirror with the silver ovals marked on
> my face, there was no way to calculate the
> dimensions of my disease, the *degree* of my
> negrophobia.

Roiling with the tumultuous effect of a storm cloud, curls of smoke rush toward the ceiling and condense into the APPARITION of a nude teenage girl. Her thatch of pubic hair is trimmed into a fuzzy, heart-shaped valentine.

> **BUBBLES**
> *(v.o.)*
>
> I formed spheres of light and color on the screen
> of my mind's eye, which I then projected on the
> surface of the glass.

Scaled to pixie proportions, the apparition swims through the air and hovers before an oval mirror set inside an ornate bronze frame. An enlarged lynxlike eye dominates the reflection in the glass.

BUBBLES

(v.o.)

The glass swirled with smoke and flickered with
luminous, multicolored flames. The ovals began
to undulate and change shape, transforming into
a silver-scaled serpent swallowing its tail.

The apparition jackknifes into the reflected eye's dilated
pupil. The pupil contracts, and the eye refracts light in
colors from pale green to ice silver.

BUBBLES

(v.o.)

The serpent hissed and slithered in a continuous
cycle of self-cannibalization, regurgitating old
skins and regenerating new, exuding trails of
metallic red and blue light shot through with
needles of gold. Then my face changed, folding
and refolding with the geometric precision of an
origami sculpture's leaves.

In the reversed colors of a photographic negative, on the
opposite side of the image reflected in the glass, Bubbles'
face looms at a towering height with a molting snake slithering around it in the pattern of a figure eight.

BUBBLES

(v.o.)

These transformations were not the faces of lives
past, as I had thought, or the beginnings of a
protective astral shell, as I had hoped, but
portents, foreshadowings of my fears.

The snake burrows under the surface of Bubbles' skin,
distorting the shape of her skull, her face folding into a
fudge-colored square with leering, froggish features. Pink
leafy patches blossom on her face, and a pair of mascara

lobster-claws frame her incandescent eyes. The spiked blond thorns crowning her chocolate skull transform into a dried-out, hightop Little Richard conk. Her incandescent eyes turn rabbit pink, redden, and glaze over with cocaine intoxication. The Little Richard conk grows into a Medusa nest of blond dreads, and the chocolate face fattens, blackens, and blisters. Ribbons of flesh flap against exposed bone. The blistered flesh knits into a large black breast and filed yellow teeth protrude from its nipple. The breast snaps its teeth and extends its tongue. The tongue swells into a large, throbbing penis. The penis sprouts a pair of bulging lemon-shaped eyes, and glow-in-the-dark dreads bloom on top of its goggle-eyed head. The penis disappears. And the lemon-shaped eyes float above a bleached nose-bone and a gold-toothed grin. Boiling like a sheet of burning plastic, the inversed reflection bleeds into a smear of colors.

BUBBLES
(v.o.)

Pulled on a current of a fine etheric substance, I
passed through the glass, and found myself
swathed in velveteen blackness. The blackness was
thick and heavy, like syrup, and shimmered with
an oil-on-water iridescence, reflecting a full
spectrum of refracted light. Its tributaries of
color converged into a black *light* of satanic
brilliance, instantly absorbing the whiteness of my
skin.

Bubbles evaporates into the combustive void, reappearing on the opposite side of the glass in black-lighted outlines.

BUBBLES
(v.o.)

Without the vampiric beauty of my whiteness,
without the definition of my skin, without my
emblematic significance, I was presence without

167

appearance, a being without basis, a creature
without context—*an invisible*—a colorless network
of organs and entrails in translucent casing.

Dropping through a series of concentric black disks, Bubbles
falls through the void as radiant and iridescent as the
blackness that surrounds her.

BUBBLES
(v.o.)

Like a sleeper losing consciousness to dreams, I
dropped through concentric, ever-widening
circles of darkness, transcending all corporal
restrictions, turning intangible, into the pure
substance of thought. Not only was I thought, I'd
become the very process of that thought—*an idea*
permutating in the web of my own capricious
thinking.

Bubbles shimmers into a polychromatic blur, her shape
shifting with symmetrical diversity.

BUBBLES
(v.o.)

As those black, hypnotic disks spun larger and
darker in the abyss, the farther and farther I fell,
confronting the contents of my own mind in full,
vivid, and animated relief, not knowing what
waited in the wellsprings of my psyche, not
knowing how I might transmogrify.

The polycrhomatic blur contracts into a narrow beam of
light, passing through the surface of the glass.

INT.—Brownstone—Bedroom—Dawn.

In CLOSE-UP, the camera follows a ray of light cast by the reflection of the candle guttering in the mirror's left-hand corner. Fine dust particles float in the beam. Slanting at a downward angle, the beam of light falls on a full-color, two-page photo in an open copy of *International Vogue*.

A shaded FINGER, pressed against the page, points to a fresh-faced BLONDE with a pair of interlocking ovals painted on her face in silver paint. Standing between TWO FEATHERED AB-ORIGINES in bright bodypaints, the silver-ovaled blonde models black Wayfarer shades; a studded, black leather jacket; and a spotted leopardskin bikini. Her abundant lemon-cream curls are tinted cotton-candy pink. The three figures stand in the cupped cotton-gloved hands of a smiling ULTRAVIOLET BLACK MAN WITH GHASTLY GREEN DREADLOCKS.

Over-the-shoulder shot of the mirror.

The color of the FACE seen in the glass is the warm cinnamon hue of a fresh-baked banana cake's crisp, sugary crust. The eyes are wildcat green. The lips are ripe and full, like pulpy citrus swollen with pungent juice. The burnished, copper-colored hair hangs in long, ropy dreadlocks, which rest on ample, upturned breasts.

As the back of her head swivels in confusion between the cinnamon-colored face in the mirror and the white face in the ad, Bubbles' face is obscured by shadow. The magazine drops to the floor, opening to:

THE UNITED COLORS OF BENETTON

A CHOIR sings in eerie tremolo offscreen. The motes of dust whirling in the beam of light reflecting off the magazine's glossy pages funnel into a spiral of cyclonic force and condense into the six-foot-tall figure of a BLACK MAN in kitchen whites, a chef's hat, and black Wayfarer shades.

With an elegant bow, the smiling Chef offers Bubbles a bowl of hot Cream of Wheat.

CREAM OF WHEAT CHEF
Is ya hongry, chile?

Close-up on Bubbles' face. There is no face. It's been replaced by a silken mesh of shadows.

Freeze-frame Cream of Wheat Chef. As the credits roll over the freeze-framed image, offscreen sounds are heard. A crowd roars in an outdoor stadium. A voice announces over the loudspeakers:

ANNOUNCER
(v.o.)

It's "Independence Day" here at Yankee Stadium. And to play "The Star-Spangled Banner," our national anthem, we present an authentic Yankee Doodle Dandy, born on the Fourth of July—*Mr. Louis Armstrong!*

The CROWD cheers. Footsteps approach the microphone. A trumpet blows the opening bars of "The Star-Spangled Banner." Then the music degenerates into a wall of abrasive, Hendrix-style feedback. The music stops and a hoarse voice says:

LOUIS ARMSTRONG
(v.o.)

Ever since I was a little boy in the streets of Orleans, I've wanted to play "The Star-Spangled

170

Banner" in the Yankees' ballpark on my birthday.
And I was refused my whole life! Now that I been
dead and buried for umpteen somethin' years,
you people come along, dig six feet down, pull
me up out of the ground, and ask me, *a dead man,*
if I'd liked to show some patriotism for my
country. Guess what you can do?

The Cream of Wheat Chef's mouth forms Louis Armstrong's
last words:

CREAM OF WHEAT CHEF
French-kiss my black New Orleans ass. DEEP.

The camera pulls back. The Cream of Wheat Chef turns
around, bends over, and drops his trousers. His ashen black
ass is whitewashed with the words:

THE END

Acknowledgments

Through the years, many have sustained me with their love, money, and couch space:

Rita Breese, Noah Seaman, Carrie Howell, Kaye Lynn Anderson, Alan Drogan, Janet Ford, Rachel Weissman, Stacye Leanza, Peter Conte, Carmine D'Intino, Lisa Blauschild, Tina Carstenson, Maria Chomentowski, Jo Ann Chapin, Gygi Jennings, Colleen Wasner, Libby Averill, Patrice Walker-Powell, Randy Boyd, Jean Bleich, and Mary Hope Lee.

Khu Cen Aton Shu Amon, Jameel Moondoc, John Farris, Rick Van Valkenberg, Emily Carter, Norman Douglas, Bernard Meisler, Patricia Winters, Tim Winkels, Mark Netter, Sabine Heredeckian, Jean J. T. Eckhoff, Josh Whalen, Debra Bergman, Butch McAdden, Tenesh Weber, Mike Zwicky, Doug McMullen, The Snow Devils, Mark Zero, Ed Morales, Erl "Dirty Ernie" Kimmich, Pam Dewey, Snoopy Best, Sheila Urbanowski, and anyone who has ever gotten me drunk in Vazac's.

Peter Dennis, Bruce Huckabey, Perry Dennis, Chuckie Williams, Ronald Williams, Tommy Williams, Charles Elbert, Paul Dennis, Patrick Dennis, Parker Dennis, Peggy Dennis, Jamal Dennis, Billy Ray Madden, Connie Madden, Gregory Madden, Stephanie James, Alexis Perkins, David Augustine, Steve Gambrell, Debra Moore, Sharon Perkins, Philip Moore, Dwayne Watts, Gail Harrison, Bennie Walker, Roscoe Carr, Craig Anderson, Jiman Brown, Preston Murray, Nathaniel Reeves, Dwayne Watts, Keith Sherrod, Mike Batts, David Reaves, Kent Bracey, Leroy Holms, and Bruce Phillips.

The New Orleans Kali Krewe, Kathy Webster, Suzanne Jones, Stephanie Jones, Frederique Pressman, Jeremy Truex, Marisa Cirasulo, Siobhan O'Neil, Jamie Delman, Jackie Geller, Diane Lourde, Elizabeth Eristoff, Tony Wagner, Paul Forbath, Jerry

Cornelius, Lynn Brownley, Michael Sullivan, Peter Firk, Kim
Walhauer, John Alpert, Sylvia Dennis, Ella James, Thomas
James, Khalid Lum, Louis Griffin, Ernst Weber, Stan
Bernstein, Neil Fandek, Michael Powell, Winston Gooden,
Keith Graham, Charles "Deal" Whitley, Etan Ben-Ami, Ian
Tannebaum, Chuck Landau, Tildy Turcherchinetz, Neil
Geraldi, Chris Gray, Wendy Anderson, Jason Dubin, Walter
Oller, Steve Assetta, Priscilla Sneff, Francois Raffoul, Elana
Seaman, Tori Leanza, Joy Sullas, Becky Nordgren, Eva
Johanos, Kerry Fristoe, Titzianna Ripani, Elena Testa, Claire
Matz, Gary "Gaz" O'Connor, and Allison Bowly.

Ed Barringer and the Communipaw Street Crew, Tracy
Morris, Bree Saulsman, Maggie Estep, Rahti Gorfien, Alexis
Gray, Lynn Tillman, Dennis Cooper, Cheryl Hardwicke,
Michael O'Donoghue, Nelson Lyon, Steve Martin, Hal Wilner,
Wes Anderson, Sheri Muhammed, Mim Udovitch, Jeff
Goldberg, Peter Donald, Jack Hasegawa, Penelope Truex, Ted
Mann, Ms. Margaret Smith, Julian Schulsberg, Lisa
Steinmeyer, Donald Suggs, Allison Goodwin, Peter Brawley,
Michael Will, Lisa Bas, Tim Beckett, Ivo "The Evil," Ian
Stephans, Cynthia Jervis, Greg 'n' Malcolm, Velcrow Ripper,
Alex Espinosa, Tyrus Coursey, Evelyn Acevedo, Joe Wood,
Theo Van Gogh, Helene Haartsman, Norman Cross, Claudio
Papilia, Helen Jardine, Tom Weatherly, Stacey Rubin, Peter
Charak, Mary Conte, Goat Carson, Jackie Carriere, Ricard
Jodoin, Norman Cross, Christine & Nick Ring, Rebecca
Korbot, Dina Petrillo, Blair Breard, Alex Pinkerson, Wadia
Gardner, Kimarie Humphries, Elaine Hines, John Moriaru,
Carl Helm, Rick Tremble, Kate Fallon, Basil "The Hook of It"
P., Kathy Horner, Herman Alves, Alba Reale, Dominic
Carlucci, Gabriella Reale, Eric Sandmark, and the gang at
Videotheque 2000 in Montreal's Saint Henri.

With extra special thanks to: Sallie Ann Glassman, Esther
Kaplan (for President, "Because America Needs a Jewish
Mother"), Dr. Steve Cannon, Catherine Texier, Joel Rose, the
Pro-Life Satanists ("Don't abort those babies, give them to
us!"), Kathy Acker, George W. S. Trow, Dan Levy, Gail Kinn,
Ruth Nolan, Mark Bradford, Faith Childs, and the New York
Foundation for the Arts.